W9-AQT-197

EQUIPMENT FOR STAGE PRODUCTION

A MANUAL OF SCENE BUILDING

By Arthur Edwin Krows

AUTHOR OF "PLAY PRODUCTION IN AMERICA,"
"PLAYWRITING FOR PROFIT," ETC.

PREFACE BY

Barrett H. Clark

AUTHOR OF "A STUDY OF THE MODERN DRAMA," ETC.

ILLUSTRATED BY THE AUTHOR

D. APPLETON AND COMPANY
New York : London : Mcmxxviii

PRINTED IN THE UNITED STATES OF AMERICA

PREFACE

Equipment for Stage Production is one of those records of experience that active men are occasionally induced as a special favor to write down for the use of other people. I'm not sure how Arthur Krows set to work preparing his MS. for publication, but I imagine it grew not according to the rules and regulations—which produce poor books when they produce anything at all—but according to the logic of his experience.

This book is in the strictest sense the result of Mr. Krows' own direct associations, and not a theoretical affair; if it had been written without skill or order it would still be useful, because the writer has set down exactly the things that he personally has seen. His association with Winthrop Ames, his fifteen years' contact with the theatre, and his first-hand knowledge of the world behind the scenes, have given him everything necessary for the preparation of such a work as he has now written.

Mr. Krows' *Play Production in America,* now for a dozen years a standard reference book which all of us who write about the theatre find it convenient to make generous use of, is, like *Equipment for Stage Production,* a work to use when you are producing, and not a book for the library. In this new work, the writer shows an even more acute sense of the practical needs of his reader than in the earlier one. His sketches, for example, were made mostly on stages where he was actually working out his own problems: they are not manufactured to fit imaginary contingencies or theoretical difficulties.

This is the sort of thing that appeals to me: Mr. Krows never puts his cart before his horse. And the strange thing about his way of attacking a job is that his book makes good reading. Baedeker's guides, which are compiled for the use of travelers, are among the most stimulating volumes in any library. Heaven knows they are unpretentious, but the House of Baedeker, because it has arrayed its facts for the convenience, comfort and entertainment of its patrons, has given us a more interesting and entertaining series of works than any arm-chair travel books I have yet seen.

Mr. Krows is in his way a Baedeker of the American theatre. He is, besides, the author of a book on playwriting, and if that art could be taught at all, his book could teach it—but since it appears for the first time almost simultaneously with this, further comment must be reserved. Meantime, here is a work for those who want to know all they need to know about the fundamentals of equipment for stage production.

Barrett H. Clark.

CONTENTS

ILLUSTRATIONS

ILLUSTRATIONS

EQUIPMENT FOR STAGE PRODUCTION

EQUIPMENT FOR STAGE PRODUCTION

CHAPTER I

THE STAGE ARRANGEMENT

IT takes a person rather well versed in ways of the theatre to become genuinely enthusiastic over an entirely empty stage. To one who knows the playhouse from only the audience side of the proscenium arch, there is nothing more disappointing than to go backstage when all known evidences of make-believe have been cleared away, and to try to recreate with his mind's eye in the gloomy, cavernous shell remaining, the magic world that he had anticipated.

To go back, on the other hand, when the orchestra still plays the exit march, and perhaps when the curtain still quivers from its descent on the closing scene —when possibly stray flutters of applause from the emptying auditorium mingle with sharp commands of division leaders and slaps of disentangled lines; when players, bright-eyed from their recent exaltation, wander toward their dressing-rooms picking their steps among the electrician's cables; when the arcs of extinguished floods and spots still glow; when everything seems to be moving at once, walls, furniture, rugs, ceilings, staircases, and all the rest, off at the sides and up somewhere into the sky—then even the casual on-looker thrills. What a change when the feverish activity of this bustling world suddenly goes dead, the lights dim abruptly to a single melancholy bulb that stands alone in the middle of the stage, when pulsing excitement has been exchanged for desolation of the tomb . . . what a change!

This book is not of the deserted theatre but of the fleeting things that constitute such evanescent glimpses of glory. It deals with the especial world of the stage crew—probably the first book confined just to them. The crew! Their name may have started with those nimble sailors who adjusted awnings over the great open amphitheatres of ancient Rome. But whatever their history, what a splendid name for those who carry audiences in ships of illusion over seas of adventure!

In the life we all know, everything depends in some degree upon everything else. So the theatre's scenery, lights and properties cannot well be what they are without commensurate things, particularly without a stage to accommodate them. Modern factors would be out of place in the theatre for which Æschylus, Euripides, and Sophocles wrote, as they would be on the stages of Shakespeare, Molière, and Sheridan. It is therefore advantageous to sketch briefly as a background of understanding, certain broad differences of these historic institutions.

The original "stage" seems to have been a simple, circular dancing place in the open air, large enough, in the instance of ancient Greece, for the evolutions of a chorus of fifty—no stage at all, in other words. The architectural background that became convenient, when the classic period had gone into decline, to suggest houses and temples on a street, seems also to have provided a narrow ledge where actors could deliver their long speeches at intervals in the choral work. This very shallow stage seems in most cases to have been about six times the width of our average proscenium arch to-day, an ample size befitting a huge auditorium required to seat a vast concourse of spectators. Performances were given only once a year, in holiday season, and always by daylight.

In Roman times the front half of the choral dancing place was reserved for spectators of importance, the portion remaining to the players being raised that the nabobs might see. In the modern sense of stage—an elevated place upon which the entire play action, of chorus and principals might be presented together—this seems to have been the real pioneer. Here again performances occurred by daylight and before vast holiday audiences who paid virtually no entrance fee.

The theatre of Shakespeare was also a daytime institution for popular patronage, but charged for admission and repeated its performances as long as the public would attend them. The stage projected well out into the audience, which therefore stood about it on three of its four sides, making impossible any serious attempt at scenic illusion. The theatre of Molière, on the other hand, was fostered by the nobility for whose convenience plays were performed indoors and often at night. His playhouse sometimes was a converted tennis court, stage at one end and with frequent attempts at painted scenery.

The real start of modern scenic illusion came in the period from about the middle of the seventeenth century to the close of the eighteenth, when the development of indoor, lighted theatres by the ruling classes, sparing neither trouble nor expense for effect, uncovered most of the working principles that are in use to-day. From the art world of Italy, especially, came the great scenic artists and stage engineers who were also the great painters and sculptors, all sustained and encouraged by munificent patronage to bend their efforts in this direction. From Italy to France and France to England the innovations traveled, acquiring other ideas as they went along, and borrowed from the court performances by the professional playhouses as rapidly as might be.

By 1800, the time of Garrick and Sheridan, there were painted drops, wings, and flats, practicable modeled pieces, footlights, top and side lights, trap-doors, counterweight systems, effects of thunder, lightning, rain, snow, and much more. Sets could be changed rapidly and often. When a theatre management could not benefit from these things, it was due to lack of funds and not lack of precedent. The nineteenth century thus started from an excellent foundation. Its theatre development continued steadily of itself and with impetus derived from progress in other lines—progress notably in lighting methods. Most important of all, of course, was the cultural development; but this was not to reach its peak in that century or, it is to be hoped, in this, either.

As far as the narrower subject here is concerned, the most striking change of the nineteenth century resulted from the sinister influence of fire. The number of playhouses increased with the growing popularity of their kinds of entertainment, and fire had made corresponding strides. In the United States alone there were recorded 176 theatre fires up to 1875. Austria was by no means the leader in the international lists; but about 1880 the awful conflagration that consumed the Ring Theatre at Vienna drew together in the so-called "Asphaleia Syndicate" a number of trained engineers with the avowed purpose first of making theatres fireproof. To build stages according to scientific principles was the secondary aim, and in achieving it these men did not invent; but they did join and bring to a forefront of attention all of the important information that Europe had to offer on stage construction.

The great pride of the Asphaleia system was that it *was* fireproof. The stage was of iron; the lines were metal cables; and the power with which the sponsors supplanted the old manual labor was water under pressure. It was objected, however, that the water brought dampness and decay to fragile materials; that the greater vibration of iron stages seriously impaired acoustical range, and as hanging canvas easily caught fire from the gas border-lights of the day, that metal cables made it impossible to cut down burning drops. The engineers also claimed for their plan certain economies in the number of stagehands required, pointing out that one operator at a board controlling the hydraulic valves could raise and lower drops and break the stage into varying levels at will; but objections to this were in the main that a few trained engineers cost more than a crew of unskilled men, while if anything went wrong the single operator at the board would be helpless. A man in each key position, working his own sets of lines and responsible for direct results, was much to be preferred. Moreover, the objectors said, breaking the stage into different levels served no real purpose because superstructures still had to be built, as in the old days, to blend them into the scene.

Discussions of this sort crossed and recrossed the frontiers of Europe and frequently reached degrees of abuse; but they had the healthful effect of bringing about some excellent compromises that may be studied in the metropolitan theatres of to-day—compromises of structure, of structural method and of building laws that must be left for expert treatment to other books of the series.

For convenience, rather than for any determination of "best stage method," the present book begins from a plan that must nevertheless be deemed worthwhile as its advantages are pointed out. This sketch, purporting to show the several parts of a good stage in their relation to each other and to the auditorium, is in its broad features the arrangement devised and executed by Winthrop Ames for his Little Theatre in New York.

The plan shown is what is known as a combination of manual labor and counterweight, admirably adapted to a small playhouse. What is first to be observed is that the whole scheme is worked out with regard to the stage manager's efficiency. His position, indicated as *A,* is at the little book-rest which is intended to hold the prompt copy of the play. Everything is arranged

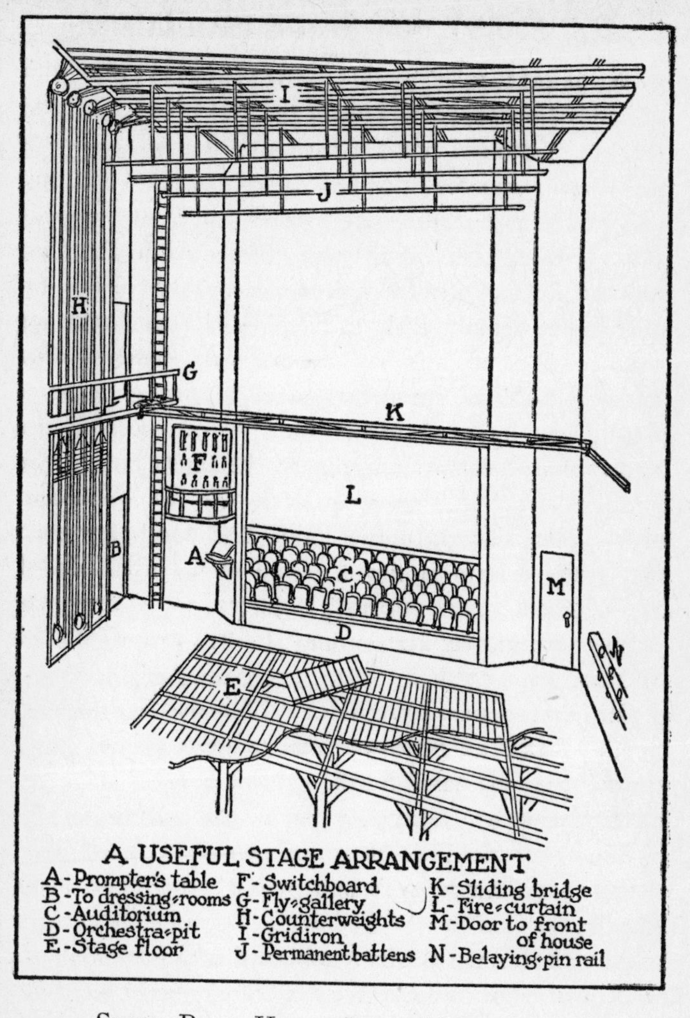

STAGE PLAN HELPS STAGE MANAGEMENT

as far as practicable for his direct communication with all departments. On a balcony just over his head stands the electrician at the switchboard. A little above the electrician is the fly-gallery where flymen work lines attached to pieces of scenery suspended from the gridiron. Looking up toward the gridiron—into the flies, as that general area over the stage and above the top of the proscenium arch is called—the stage manager may see for himself that the drops are hanging true and that the lines are working well. Through a secret opening in the wall before him, he can peep at the audience and communicate with the musicians in the orchestra pit. A similar opening for the electrician gives him view of house lights and footlights even when the curtain is down. And then, just back of the stage manager's position, is the way to the dressing-rooms that he may keep in unobstructed touch with the players.

In the necessary compactness of a theatre building, in these days of expensive real estate, it is not often practicable to have much unused space backstage. When Hartley Granville-Barker considered taking over the Booth Theatre as his own New York playhouse some years ago, and wanted the stage made deeper, he was obliged to forego that point because its back wall was also the back wall of the Shubert Theatre, facing the other way. What is more often true is that the back wall is on the next street and therefore, of course, cannot be moved outward. This, however, has special advantages. To have the stage doors on the back street is highly convenient, for example; but in small theatres that do not cut through the block, this is not always possible. At the Little Theatre in its original form—before its auditorium was enlarged and turned with the stage in another direction—the door for the players was in the lobby, connected with the stage by means of a separate passageway. There was no large door for the scenery, as is customary; but scenery going out crossed the footlights and the auditorium and then reached the street through double doors in the foyer.

It is not often possible to have much space even at the sides of the stage, in the wings. The sensible solution of this difficulty has been not to share the available space side and side alike, but to throw most of it to one or the other, with the main labor facilities grouped there. This "working side" as it is called, is therefore the area of most continuous activity backstage, with its busiest part, clearly indicated in the sketch, "downstage," close to the proscenium arch. In the older theatres the space here shown at either side of the arch and manifestly so useful was generally lost or used as cloakroom for the proscenium boxes. The architects to-day realize that, as seats for the audience must spread out somewhat fanwise from the arch, the outlying space close to the arch may be included to advantage as part of the stage. It would be no good for seats anyway, as no spectator in that position could see the play.

The working side is generally kept as clear as possible, so the more room is required to store heavy properties and pieces of scenery that cannot be hung in the flies. The less-used side consequently is devoted in the main to temporary storage, although its reduced room precludes much of that. For storage purposes the rear of the stage is preferred, including the back of the working side, where, to make packing easier, the height of the fly-gallery is nicely calculated to clear the tops of any ordinary pieces of scenery placed beneath it. When the number of properties and scene pieces is very large, it often happens that the supply overflows into the alley or the street where tarpaulins protect what has been crowded out. At the Metropolitan Opera House in New York there is a regular outside niche for just such emergencies. Another scheme—an old Belasco method—is to lower bulky pieces through the stage into the cellar or dock beneath, a fairly simple solution because, as will be noted, the stage floor is removable in sections as required, anywhere in the acting zone.

CHAPTER II

CURTAINS, DROPS AND BORDERS

ANY distinction between curtains and drops is rather loose. The difference, such as it is, lies between those hangings that close off the proscenium arch itself, in whole or in part, and those that may more especially be denominated scenery; but to the casual eye they are pretty much identical.

The outermost curtain is the one that must be of an area sufficient to close the proscenium arch, so it is the largest of the front curtains. The law takes special cognizance of it and determines its nature because it is primarily a fire precaution. It is designed instantly to seal the stage opening in event of a blaze on the illusion side. Fire originating on the audience side of the footlights is exceedingly rare. The fire curtain sometimes is made of iron or steel plates riveted together; but as this makes a rather unwieldy affair, with problems of expense and deterioration, preference is given to what is commonly called the asbestos drop. It is a piece all by itself. To accommodate it, the proscenium arch is slotted at top and sides. In this channel it moves, independent of all the other drops in the theatre.

In time of fire the height of the average stage becomes a veritable flue, especially because above the stage is a large ventilator, instantly opened by the parting of fusible links, to clear the air of smoke. Sealing the proscenium opening stops the draft that otherwise fans the flames. What is more important in many ways than confining the fire to the stage is to keep the audience from seeing it or sensing in any way the alarm connected with it, because the horror of such conflagrations has come more from panic than from the burning. For the same reason fire engines coming to a theatre are always sparing of bell and whistle.

Having an asbestos curtain is an excellent provision. And yet, although the Iroquois Theatre in Chicago was so equipped, it had one of the worst playhouse fires in living memory. The asbestos curtain there was even released in time; but it stuck midway in the arch and only increased the panic. To-day the very sensible law in most places is that the asbestos curtain shall be lowered at least once during every performance. Thereby its emergency operation is assured.

Entering now upon the scene proper, one leaves "curtains" and encounters "drops." Drops are painted cloths or gauzes of varying widths, suspended from the gridiron, and all, with one exception, reaching to the floor of the stage. The exception is the "half-leg" drop which is in the main an abbreviated overhead piece but that descends at one or more points to join real columns, rounded tree-trunks or other imitation pieces that thus connect it with the ground. In the "leg" drop the columns are part of the drop. When a cloth does not relate directly or in this way to the floor of the scene, but is just a strip held in air, it is called a "border." Drops are commonly used for large painted perspectives in exterior scenes, where also occur most of the borders that in their turn sometimes represent overhead foliage but that always primarily prevent front-row spectators from seeing too far upward into the flies. Narrow drops are sometimes employed as "backings" to be viewed through windows or doors.

As the largest drop in the front is the fire curtain, the largest in the back of the stage is the "cyke"—the cyclorama. This also is in a class by itself. Its purpose is to represent the sky; and there is so much of this huge cloth that it frequently reaches nearly to the gridiron and curves around forward at the sides of the scene almost to the curtain-line. Its color is in most instances a pale blue and sometimes a dead white, sky effects being obtained by projecting colored lights upon it. It commonly is laced into position to pull all the wrinkles out of it. The size of the cyclorama makes its extended movement impracticable; but to get it as much as possible out of the way when not in use, it occasionally is raised just high enough for backstage folk to walk under it, while the side pieces are gathered in. Certain of the larger theatres of Europe have another plan which is to keep the cyclorama wound, when not in use, on a tall, slender drum at one side of the stage, ready to be pulled out into place at short notice. Still another way is to suspend it from a curved track, such as is used frequently for garage doors. The cyclorama serves the same purpose as the plaster or concrete "dome horizon," but has the greater advantage of portability. The dome feature, which, as its name implies, carries the "sky" forward overhead, tends to interfere with hanging pieces in the flies and is said seriously to affect acoustics.

Front curtains are made to disclose what is behind them in several ways. They may be lifted bodily into the flies, as they usually are; they may be rolled, as they used to be in minor theatres where there was insufficient space over the stage; they may reverse common procedure by sinking into a slot along the curtain-line, as was long done at the New York Hippodrome and as is sometimes done for open-air stages; they may part in the middle and slide off at the sides, or they may loop back. Additional novelty forms are unimportant. The fire curtain, being necessarily of a single piece and its material rather stiff, preferably is lifted bodily into the flies. This means that the height of the flies must in that case be about double the height of the proscenium arch that the fire curtain fills.

To clear the arch fully, however, is rarely necessary. Very seldom does any theatre present a scene so lofty that it requires the full height of the opening. At the same time the height is usually there should occasion demand it. But if this is a valid reason for lifting the fire curtain out of sight, it should also apply to the "act drop" that comes next. Nevertheless, the act drop—which as the name indicates is used to mark beginnings and ends of acts—is usually hung from a point lower than the fire curtain employs, and could not be drawn all the way up without having its rigging changed. No example of such alteration is on the convenient records. Settings are almost invariably wider than high, while the ordinary proscenium arch is higher than wide. Why, then, should the act drop

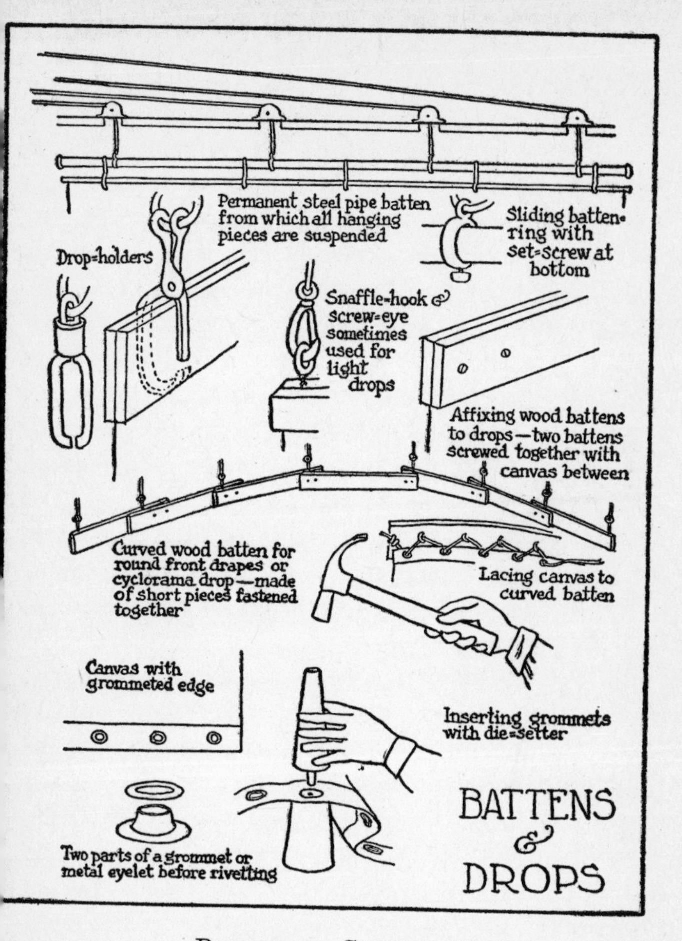

REMOVABLE CURTAINS

The secret is in the batten and in the devices for fastening it to the permanent rigging. The simplest batten is two strips of wood screwed together with the curtain edge between. The strips are usually scarved, the better to grip the cloth.

go so far up out of the picture frame? With the fire curtain it is different because there the function is different, and its special rigging would be exceedingly difficult to alter.

The artistic eye has been prompt to resent the unattractiveness of a flat curtain not fully withdrawn from the frame; and in the very large theatres (and in vaudeville theatres commonly to-day), that upper area used to be covered with a special cloth painted often to represent festooned crimson velvets tied back with golden cords. This piece has long been known, consequently, as "the grand drapery."

As settings vary in height so also do they differ in width. In the old days, however—that is to say nearly a century ago—the width was rather arbitrarily fixed for all scenes. In actual dimensions a bedroom and a ballroom set were pretty much the same. This was just one of the conventions of the theatre of the time, involving existing conditions of sight-lines, lighting and acoustics. It was accepted readily enough by audiences. When improving conditions gradually made the picture-frame stage possible and plays became consequently more realistic in theme and treatment, authoritative voices were raised to question the fixed size of the stage opening. One of the most insistent was that of the eminent artist, Hubert von Herkomer, who, toward the close of the nineteenth century, conducted an experimental theatre in conjunction with his school of art at Bushey, on the outskirts of London. For that little playhouse he devised an adjustable proscenium, contending that to have a rigid one was as absurd as using one-size frames for all paintings.

The adjustable proscenium is scarcely practical; but its intention is commendable enough. To achieve the same purpose—even before Herkomer's time—theatres generally had added two simple masking pieces that could be slid on, one at either side, to any reasonable distance. Variations in height were met in the simple, obvious way by stopping the lifted curtain in mid-air, marking the curtain-rope to guide the man backstage who hauled it up, with the additional safeguard from prying eyes of a strip of cloth across the front of the scene at top. The two convenient side pieces are still known by their traditional name, "tormentors," and the top strip, probably by analogy, is called "the teaser." Constituting thus a sort of inner proscenium, tormentors and teaser are commonly given an artistic treatment all their own, painted columns and draperies being routine forms.

Draw-curtains, which is to say those that divide in the middle and pull away at the sides, must first of all have something upon which to slide. Whatever it is, it may be supported only in the middle, where the curtains part, and at the ends, where they stop. It must be rigid enough in the unsupported places not to sag with the weight of the curtains, and yet slender enough to permit them to glide easily. A common solution is a metal pipe at least an inch in diameter; but probably there is nothing simpler, and generally easier to adjust and readjust, than a metal cable drawn absolutely taut by turnbuckles at the ends.

The track, whether pipe or cable stretched on turnbuckles, does not support the curtains directly. Curtain-rings intervene. Here again is a device familiar in most households; but curtain-rings come in such astounding variety in these inventive days, that a description of one well-adapted to the present purpose is not misplaced. A single ring, sewn fast to the top of the curtain, and ample enough to encompass the aforesaid cable or pipe—and also the draw-lines, which will be described presently—is a fairly practicable and common unit. A much better form, however, that keeps its several functions separate is in three parts. A top ring slides on the cable; a second ring below that accommodates the draw-lines, and a hook still lower engages with a small ring sewn to the curtain. The last-named ring and hook make possible the detachment of the curtain without disturbing the rigging proper—a convenience greatly to be appreciated in practice. In all events, whatever form the curtain-ring happens to take, it should be selected in size generous enough not to bind on the track and draw-lines when the curtain moves.

Particular care should be exercised that binding is not induced by the manner in which the ring is fastened to the curtain. Some of the patent rings have the parts that attach to the curtain mounted on swivels so that one cannot twist the other out of line; but failing this, and particularly when the curtains have their own little rings to be hooked to the traveling parts, the edge of the curtain should be sewn in such relationship to the rings—either longitudinally or crosswise—that friction will be reduced to the minimum. Rings are usually sewn to a curtain at intervals of one foot.

The ordinary "handy-man" can make of the draw-

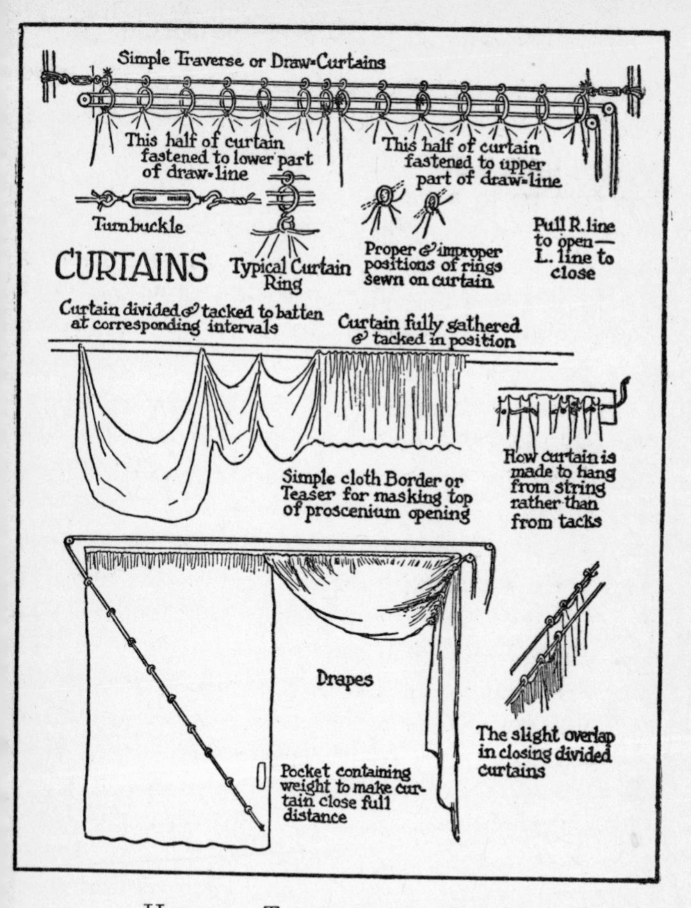

HANGING TRAVERSES AND DRAPES

The method of hanging pleated curtains and borders is given. The common turnbuckle, shown in the illustration, is one of the most useful devices in curtain rigging. With light steel cables it makes a simple, convenient and entirely dependable construction.

lines for this type of curtain one of the most complicated systems ever devised. Yet, in the professional theatre, there is probably no simpler rigging. A single line goes up to a pulley at one side of the curtains, crosses over through the rings to a pulley at the other side, returns through the rings again to a third pulley, close to the first one, and so down to the stage floor. One curtain is fastened to the upper part of the line as it goes in one direction through the rings; the other to the lower as it comes back. Both curtains are thus operated from the same side of the stage. Pull one end of the line to open; the other to close. The ends are marked to distinguish them.

The curtains are permanently fastened at the sides. As the rings slide with the curtains, the fastenings to the draw-lines are made to them. Each curtain has its first and third ring thus attached—no more than those. The first ring would and does ordinarily suffice; but including the third brings smoother movement, divides the strain and makes doubly sure of the pull when it is needed. To bring the lower edges of the curtain together in closing, they are generally weighted with a couple of small pieces of lead. If the curtains are closed smartly, these lower ends will then join without trouble.

As to pulleys, it is highly essential to use a shielded kind that will keep the line on the wheel, or sheave. The line itself should fit these conditions and should be uniform in size throughout its length, without bindings or splices or anything else that may possibly interfere with action. The good sense of this is manifest. For the light curtains, common in smaller theatres, what are known as awning-pulleys and their corresponding lines are excellent.

In actually hanging the curtain, it is made to clear the floor by a couple of inches. Condition of the atmosphere has much to do with the length. In damp weather the cloth hangs down noticeably; it shortens with dry heat. Much depends, too, on the desired appearance of the closed curtain. If it is to hang in folds instead of flat, the top must be pleated to provide that effect; and there must be a correspondingly greater amount of material to double-up. The pleats must be made evenly. As they will occur, probably, to match the number of curtain-rings, one pleat to a ring—giving the ring that much more of a hold—the cloth must be divided accordingly.

In draw-curtains the pleats naturally must be sewn in place; but the manner of dividing the length easily to find where they should go, is not vastly different from the method employed in hanging drape, or loop, curtains, where the top is immovable, or in fastening a pleated cloth border to mask the top of the proscenium opening. The last-named course of procedure is illustrated herewith.

The long wooden batten, to which the border is attached, is marked off into halves, quarters, eighths, sixteenths, and possibly thirty-seconds. The cloth is, of course, much longer than the batten, for it must allow for gathering. Nevertheless, it is marked off, in accordance with its own length, into halves, quarters and the rest. The ends of the cloth are tacked to the ends of the batten. Then the middle cloth-mark is tacked to the middle batten-mark, the quarters to the quarter-marks and the sixteenths to sixteenths, this scheme being pursued until all corresponding marks have been joined. The result is that only short intervals remain; and they may be divided easily by gauging with the eye. Of course, a pleat or part of one—depending on the elaborateness of the plan—is made each time a tack is put in. The ordinary way is just to double a pinch of cloth under for each tack.

Now, a tack is not a very secure fastening for ordinary cloth which tears away so easily. But it is assumed that the cloth is duly reënforced by doubling, hemming, or binding the edge. To relieve the strain further, a stout cord is sometimes run through the top of the curtain with a sail-needle; and the tacking is done then in such way that the tacks support the cord and the cord supports the curtain.

Drape-curtains, as their name implies, are the sort that just loop back at the sides. They have their points of merit, but probably are much less practical than traverses. For one thing, they tend to fill up useful space in the proscenium opening; for another, the wear and tear on them is great; for a third they interfere with lights and cast troublesome shadows; for a fourth they gather and stir up a lot of dust in a very awkward place. In professional theatres they are used mostly for ornamental effect in the ceremonies of opening and closing performance, leaving the more practical work of dividing the acts to simple drops.

Drapes are tacked as desired to a fixed batten at top, and also fastened, as a rule but not necessarily, down the sides. They are made to overlap three or four inches; and one is weighted near the bottom so that it will flap across its mate in closing. In the simplest form they are worked from the same side of the stage by two lines, one to each drape. For the near curtain a line runs over a pulley, at the upper outside corner, and thence down through a row of rings to usually three or four feet above the lower inside corner where it is fastened. When the line is pulled, the curtain obviously is looped up and away. For the far curtain the same method is employed, save that the line is carried from its pulley, at the upper corner, across the stage and down over another pulley to where the operator stands. To obtain the most effective loop requires careful figuring and experiment. No hard-and-fast rule may be given because much depends on the relative dimensions of the proscenium opening and the bulk of the stuff in the curtains. In some large examples two and three lines are used on each drape to make an extra number of loops.

It is difficult to prevent the mark of the line from showing in time on the front of the drape, the sooner if the curtain material is soft and light. The two outstanding precautions to offset that are to put a diagonal reënforcing strip along where the line goes, and to exercise care in sewing the rings to the drape at an angle that will facilitate the line's free movement.

The old-fashioned rolled curtain is pretty much relegated to the museum. Years ago, metropolitan stars *en tour* with their productions often were obliged to play in small-town "opera houses" where the stages had no flies. There simply was no room to hang drops in the approved manner; and rolling them up was the simplest solution. It never was a good way. If the curtain is a painted one (and it usually was in that period) the surface soon shows smudges and signs of wear. In the interest of completeness only, an accompanying illustration shows how such curtains were managed.

The folding "French" curtain, familiar from its use as a fancy shade in certain shop-windows, is another form that is not especially practical. The curtain here is just hauled up in a bunch like the sail of a ship—although a sail collapses down, not up—which, indeed, may have suggested it. To accomplish this, a series of vertically descending lines are fastened at intervals to the bottom of the curtain; and, as in the case of the drapes, each line is run through a number of rings fastened to the cloth. When the lines are pulled up simultaneously, the top of the curtain being fixed, the drop is, of course, crushed together.

For a lifting curtain like the act drop, that does not have to be removed from its place, the sides are frequently reënforced with curtain-guides, little spool affairs, clamped not only to the top and bottom battens but at intervals down the edge of the canvas. They run up and down, with the curtain, on fixed cables that extend from the floor up into the flies. They are especially useful in preventing the curtain from swaying in drafts.

A multiplicity of lines occurs in hanging the French curtain; but the backstage sailor has simplified their working no less than his brother on the sea has mastered his. He has ways of reducing a dozen or so lines to just one or two actually to be handled. Some of those ways are indicated here. When the lines have gone

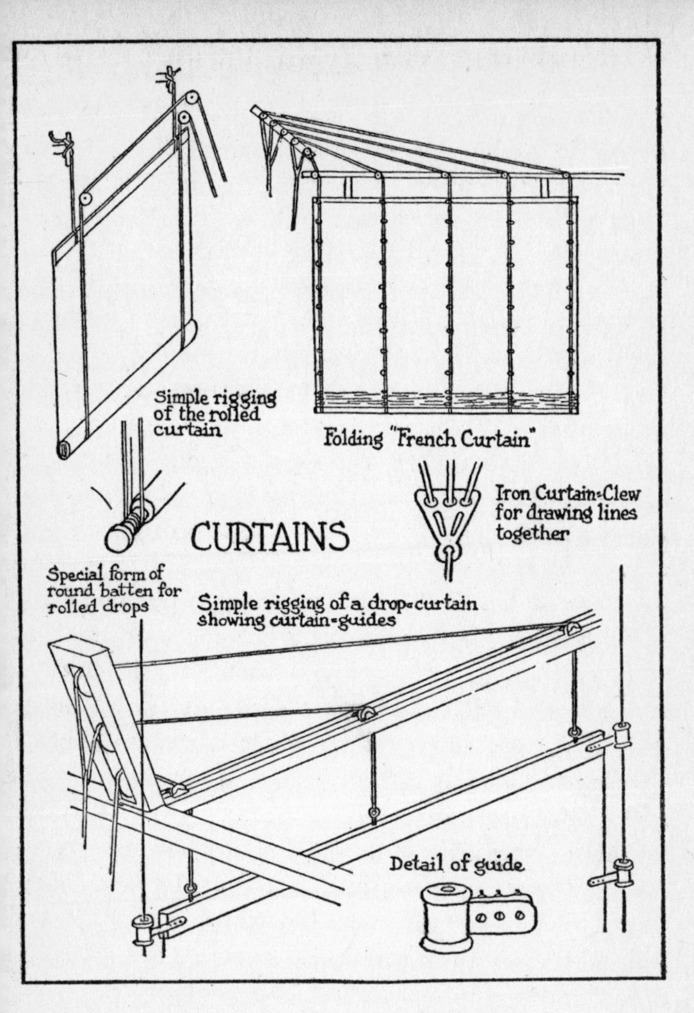

Overhead Curtain Rigging

The rolled curtain is a form originally devised for use where there was insufficient room above to lift it up bodily. It has virtually disappeared.

through their systems of pulleys as far as they will go, they are joined as convenient. Sometimes the ends are merely spliced, although this is rarely satisfactory because some of the lines slacken or tighten and therefore cannot pull evenly. To meet this problem is presented a convenient device called the curtain-clew. In its top may be fastened and separately adjusted as many lines as required; in the bottom is tied the one line that continues thence down to the operator on the stage level. Where just a couple of lines come together to be carried on as one, the rigger sometimes contrives them of a single, continuous piece, merely looping the lower line over it. The two original lines then keep their respective lengths automatically adjusted by sliding back and forth through the loop.

With the lifting curtain the gridiron comes into the scope of inquiry. The gridiron looks very much like its namesake. It consists of a series of open beams, with transverse supports, the whole nowadays almost always of iron or structural steel. It spreads, within just a few feet of the top of the flies, over virtually the entire stage. From this grating are suspended virtually all hanging pieces used in the world behind the scenes. There is a difference of opinion as to whether the beams should run lengthwise or across for greatest strength; but the final answer to this must rest with engineering experts in stress and strain.

On the "grid," from the proscenium arch to the back wall, are rows of pulleys, usually built into the frame, each row or set running from side to side of the stage. Over these pulleys run lines to support the hanging pieces. The lines do not hang free; but each set is attached to a permanent batten, usually a metal pipe—and from this the given piece of scenery is suspended. These permanent battens are so trim and convenient that the old plan, of fastening sandbags to the lines when not in use, is rapidly going out of fashion.

Properly to lift the batten and its freight, the pulleys or blocks in each set must be strictly in a row. To avoid consequent entanglement of the lines as they come through to the top of the grid, and make their way to the working side of the stage, the corresponding pulleys at that side are placed usually one above another in what is called a sloping head-block. To these pulleys the lines rise from the gridiron blocks in long, low diagonals without interference and with complete economy of space. The head-block is made to lean or slope over the working side, so that as the lines continue their way down toward the stage floor, or the fly-gallery, they are kept separate in the same way.

The minimum number of lines to a stage drop is three, with five common on the larger metropolitan stages. The three are known respectively, and rather obviously, as the "middle," the "long" and the "short" lines. This mode of rigging facilitates adjustment of the "trim" or "hang" of the drop. The two extra lines, where five is the rule, are merely to sustain the extra weight.

It is a very small stage indeed, and probably a very inexpertly managed one, where the full labor of raising and lowering drops is done by unaided muscle power. The action of counterpoises is too well known and too readily available not to be used. In the simplest professional form of counterweighting, a sandbag is merely attached to the curtain-clew, thus balancing much of the "heft" of the drop or whatever the freight may be. The stage sandbag is best made of heavy canvas stoutly laced and with a hook on it; but best things are not always used in the theatre any more than they are anywhere else. A bunch of sash-weights bound with a bit of wire is just as apt to serve if the stagehands have nothing better handy. Still, there is really no more objection to the sash-weights than to the sandbag, for what unfavorable criticism there is is directed toward all dangerously heavy objects dangling overhead. Even sandbags have been known to break loose on high and do serious damage in landing.

An up-to-date stage has its counterpoises partly sealed in chutes along the wall of the working side. They are much like the "chest-weights" in a gymnasium, only, of course, very much larger. To make the balance complete, the weight may be increased or diminished by regulating the number of iron blocks on the carriage, just as sand may be added to or taken from the sandbag in the old plan. The lines from the batten are attached to the top of the weighted carriage. So also is the curtain-rope, which goes on up over a pulley, at the edge of the gridiron, and comes down again beside the operator. The operator therefore really pulls the counterweight up and down; and the counterweight in turn pulls the batten and its freight up and down.

To fasten the lines to the permanent metal batten, the batten is provided with rings that may be slid

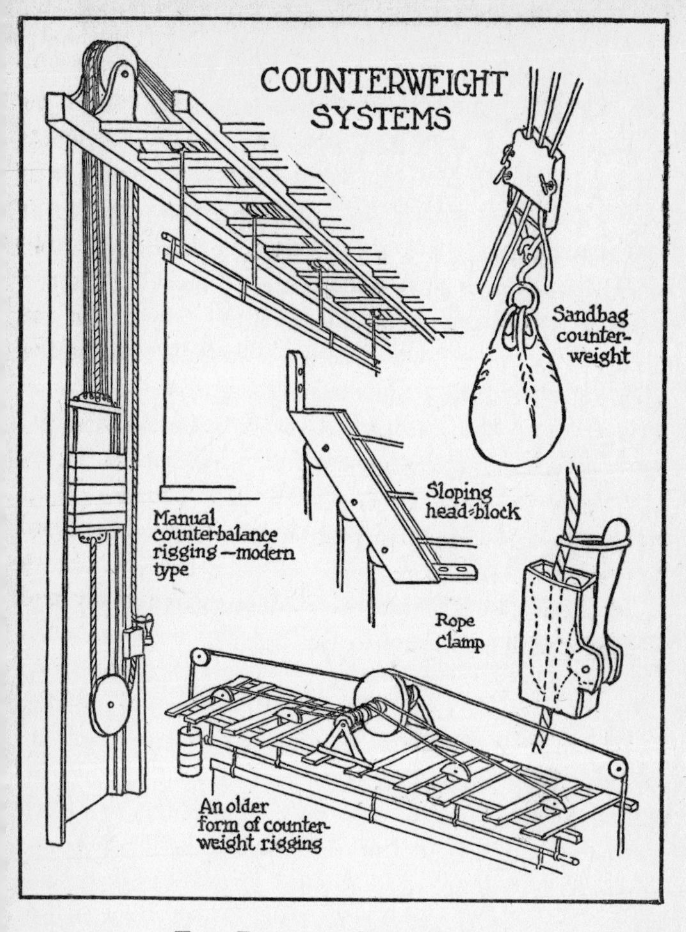

THE BALANCE SAVES LABOR

In stage practice the counterweight principle makes it possible to lift the heaviest pieces with slight effort. It is one of the oldest mechanical aids in the world of illusion, having been used extensively in Italy and France in the seventeenth century.

along, to the desired points of attachment, and there made fast with set-screws. To fasten the batten to a drop requires other devices; and they come in many ingenious forms, as Patent Office reports attest. The drops already have wooden battens attached to them top and bottom. The drop-holders, consequently, are all contrived to engage with those. The time-honored method of tying a drop (and a pretty barbarous one it is) is to punch holes in the canvas, just under the wooden batten, and run the ropes through. For a very light drop, heavy screw-eyes, in the top, with bits of rope passed through them, may serve to tie it; or they may be made to engage with snaffle-hooks, or "snap-hooks," already in place on the permanent metal batten. But the more approved drop-holders, shown in the illustration, catch the wooden batten easily and securely without injury to the canvas.

CHAPTER III

THE BOX SET

This present progressive century was well begun before all theatres had relinquished the old practice of representing closed rooms with open wings and borders. In the earlier time a side wall was only suggested with three or more wing-pieces ranged like shutters—as, indeed, they were sometimes called—one behind another from the curtain-line to the back drop. The ceiling was also a mere idea, a corresponding number of borders painted usually to represent overhead beams. The outstanding difference of modern scenery is said to be its employment of suggestion as opposed to literal representation; but in the old days suggestion was about all there was to it. Even doors and windows, in the back "wall," were mere slender frames fastened to the drop, with flimsy moving parts that would not bear much handling.

Of course it was not scenic suggestion in the best latter-day sense, which indicates a sound, fine, artistic principle; but it was not literal representation either. It was because it was such a sorry, unsatisfactory attempt at being literal that it now seems so pitiful. In the improved stage lighting of a later time it called attention to itself by being so poorly done.

As living conditions improved, with civilization's march, the public's insistence on greater verisimilitude in scenery was easier met by stage producers. One kept pace with the other. The circumstances were bound together, as, in fact, they still are. So in 1841, when Dion Boucicault caused a sensation by using, at the première of his play "London Assurance," what is said to have been the first "box" or "sealed" setting, with continuous side-walls and ceiling, the innovation must be judged as something that grew naturally out of the times. The greatest single producing cause was, perhaps, the gas lighting that had come into use only about twenty years before (electricity did not come into the theatre till about 1882), superseding oil, and candles before that. With the scenic makeshifts then revealed in a comparatively bright illumination, it is not surprising that spectators demanded better stage counterfeits of the real world that they knew for themselves and could therefore judge in comparison.

Important theatres were quick to adopt the sealed setting; but in minor playhouses the old method lingered for more than half a century. Here again it was a matter neither of simple inclination nor of prejudice. The lesser theatres were equipped on the older plan and could not well afford revolutionary changes of installation. They were lucky if they inherited the discarded equipment of the first-class houses. Moreover, gas was not at once available to them all, and as long as they had the old lighting the obsolete subterfuges did very well.

From the beginning the unit of construction in the box setting has been the simple screen—a light wooden frame, braced as necessary and covered over. The covering most of the time has been canvas, especially because it is light, but also because it is surprisingly durable. Just as the Eskimo can float in his skin-covered oomiak on a sea of broken, jagged ice, that no rigid construction could withstand, so the canvas screen, or "flat," emerges intact after incredible abuses. But there are other coverings, including the paper surfaces that once came out of Italy, and the composition "wall-boards" so successfully adopted in late years by motion picture studios.

Lightness is demanded not only for easy moving around the stage but for transportation on the road. Productions *en tour* must also consider size, for all their scene pieces must be able to go through the comparatively small door of a baggage car. Consequently, large flats are made to fold, usually in two parts but sometimes in three, with the painted surfaces inward to protect them. Hooks and screw-eyes on the edges keep them together while traveling, or sometimes light nails are driven through temporarily for the same purpose. Oftener than not they just keep themselves together. Where touring limitations need not be observed, as in a repertory or stock theatre, an ampler, heavier construction may be used. Builders there also may indulge in the economy of having flats covered on both sides—double-faced, like Janus. Reversible flats have disadvantages, however, one being that they are more difficult to join for continuous walls, and another that the necessity of handling their surfaces to move them makes them soil much more rapidly than the single-faced type.

The back wall of the setting has long been constituted, of course, by the back drop. Side walls might conceivably be made in the same fashion if hanging a drop from front to back would not interfere with overhead pieces, hanging transversely, and their systems of lines. At the same time there are especial cases, principally those demanding quick changes, wherein side and back walls have all been suspended together in the flies. Nowadays even the back drop has been supplanted in the interior setting, its successor being a large flat that is, nevertheless, hung just as a drop would be.

Closing in the ceiling requires a method all its own. The ceiling-piece is just a large flat that is kept hanging vertically in the flies until required. While the stage is still clear, it is lowered until it rests on the floor, at which time a ring at the bottom is attached to a line which draws it up until the ceiling-piece hangs just a trifle higher than its intended final position. Walls are then joined beneath it; and, when they are ready, the piece is dropped upon them and made fast. To meet touring conditions involving stages of varying widths and depths, the ceiling-piece is commonly made to overhang the walls generously. For the same reason walls are often made that they may be telescoped or pulled out at practicable points. This method of adjustment is a simple one, and requires little emphasis as a building "secret." It is a mere accommodation of one setting to many stages, and in the larger houses particularly—where for a setting of fixed size the tormentors would have to be closed in over the gaps—makes it possible for spectators at the extreme sides to see.

Doors, windows, mantels and the like, are still some-

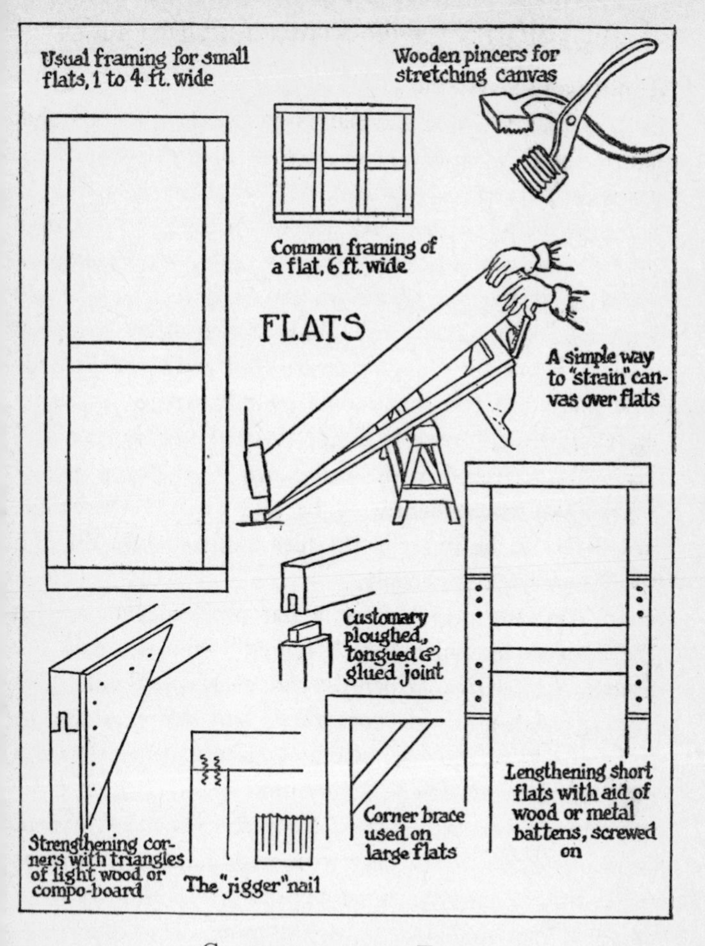

CONSTRUCTION OF FLATS

Rigidity is highly important, and so is lightness. Stretching the canvas is not as difficult as may appear, for, after it is tacked and glued into place over the edges, it is shrunk and made taut by the application of ordinary glue size.

times painted on the surface or lightly fastened to it; but in best practice the flat is cut with openings that allow for their insertion as separate pieces. One of the most important advantages of this scheme is that a window being opened, or a door closed, in its own frame, will not noticeably jar the make-believe, canvas walls, a serious and much-ridiculed defect of the old scenery. Quivering walls have often been banished in late years by using flats covered with wall-board; but there are too many obvious advantages in using canvas, while, properly used, it need not quiver. A large flat covered with wall-board is a pretty heavy affair, not conveniently to be slid around the stage, not safely to be hung in the flies and not light enough to be transported cheaply.

In attaining rigidity for a flat much depends upon the manner in which it is "framed"—that is, how the frame is made over which the canvas is stretched. This frame must not twist or warp, and yet it must be light for easy moving, while it should be made of a soft wood that may be nailed and out of which nails may be drawn without splitting it. The last-named requirement is fairly easy to meet; and the consensus of feeling about the most appropriate wood narrows down to seasoned, clean, white pine or spruce, free from knots. But the other requirements demand expert joinery.

For virtually all framing, large and small, lumber three inches wide and seven-eighths of an inch thick is the rule. The corners are grooved and tongued, or sometimes doweled, and then glued under clamps. The same is preferably done with the cross-pieces. Frames made in this way will stand much knocking-about and will keep their shape for years. Most amateur builders miter the corners, which is probably the worst way of all. A miter is exceedingly useful for certain purposes —although it is usually tongued or "feathered" even in picture-frames—but it is notoriously a weak joint, and in stage building soon proves itself poorly adapted to even ordinary requirements.

If the frame is a very large one, extra cross-pieces are inserted at likely places and the corners are re-enforced in various ways. Strengthening with the so-called "jigger-nail" is one way, but it invites contempt from the conscientious carpenter. He prefers to set in little diagonal braces, not across the back but inside the frame. At times he will tolerate small triangles of "compo-board" nailed over the corners; but certainly the inner braces make the better job. Outside reënforcement is, of course, impracticable if the flat is to be double-faced.

The frame, duly made, must be covered with canvas. If the canvas comes in strips too narrow to cover —a width of two yards is perhaps commonest—two or more must be joined. They may be sewn, as they would be in the sail of a ship, but the established and best way to do this is to overlap them and glue the edges with carpenter's glue, because that makes an evener surface. Seams generally run opposite to the "pull," which is to say horizontally across the piece. That accomplished, the end is next tacked and glued to one edge of the frame, and finally pulled, or "strained," as they used to call it in the old studios, over the other edges, where it is also glued and tacked.

For the sake of even pull, the warp and woof of the material should run, respectively, squarely with the top and sides of the flat. In the process a wooden pincers is a useful tool; but a metal pincers, with its jaws wrapped in cloth, has its own merits.

But all flats are not for interior settings. The exterior setting, which remains the greatest problem for the scenic artist because of the number of planes he is obliged to consider in it, uses the flat in many forms. The most familiar form is that of the "wing," the piece that is used to mask the side of the scene and that is painted ordinarily to represent trees or tall shrubbery. Another is what is called the "profile strip" or "cut-out," frequently seen as a hedge, across the road, or as a row of distant hills, resting on the stage floor—an intermediate line of distance between the acting zone and the back drop.

These pieces present special difficulties in having uneven edges; the wing has leaf-forms, with little spaces cut out, and the hills have their contours. However, the framing in either case is comparatively simple. The builder conceives the body of the piece as a simple rectangle or square or whatever other plane geometrical figure it may suggest, and builds the frame accordingly. The uneven edge is built on. Using compoboard, or one of the many wall-boards that may be shaped easily with a jig or compass-saw, he builds it out from the frame proper, strengthening it as necessary with minor braces. When the whole is then covered with canvas, glued to the extension parts, the uneven edge is cut out according to the design.

The wing-piece for an exterior setting is usually

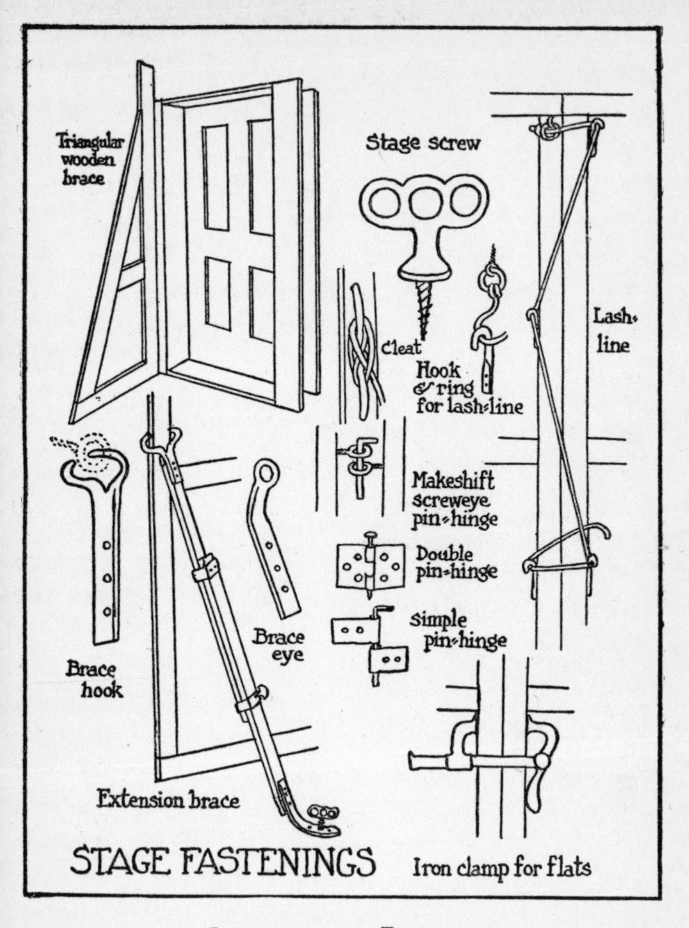

Joinings and Bracings

There are shown here the four most useful fastenings back-stage, the stage-brace, the lash-line, the stage-screw and the clamp. Of especial interest is the triangular wooden brace, hinged to the door frame and swung outward.

made as a "two-fold," hinged in two parts and opened at an angle like an ordinary folding screen, so that it stands alone. If it is very tall, a small extra section, possibly not more than a couple of feet high and called a "flipper," is hinged to one of the two larger parts and turned at another angle to give the whole a steadier base. That is not all that secures the wing, however. There is, in addition, the excellent "stage-brace."

A stage-brace may be just a stick propped against the flat and nailed at one end to the flat and at the other to the stage floor. The stage floor is adapted also to such treatment. Incidentally, it may be mentioned that when the stagehand nails a prop in that manner, he doesn't drive the nail all the way in, but leaves enough of the head for the claw of his hammer, that he carries on his hip, to pull out again.

Then there is the development of the stage-brace into a patent form. Its first feature here is that it consists of two or more sticks sliding upon each other so that the device may be adjusted to any reasonable length and fixed there with thumb-screws. At the upper end is a double hook that may be slipped over one of the strips comprising the frame of the flat, and made to hold it tightly when the brace is twisted down to the floor, or that may be engaged with an eye attached to the flat. At the lower end is an iron "heel" with a hole in it; and through the hole a stage-screw (shown here in illustration) may be forced into the floor. One of the more recent patents provides a "rocker heel" (reminiscent of Old Jim Crow, celebrated in the annals of minstrelsy)—a curved affair that gives better hold to the stage-screw irrespective of the angle at which the brace is set. Patent braces are made in sizes that range from one that may be extended from two to about four feet, to a big fellow that is twelve feet long when closed and nearly twenty-three feet when opened.

There are many other forms of brace designed for especial purposes. There is the "floor-stay" for leg-drops—a flat bar, fastened to the floor as required with a stage-screw, and having a raised, curved end to clamp over the bottom batten of the drop. There are the "saddle-irons," light steel affairs to frame and thereby to strengthen openings cut in flats for doors, windows and the like. There are the "pivot-jacks" to support certain doors and gates and long French windows as they swing open and closed, strong and yet easily fixed in position with the omnipresent stage-screw.

The stranger behind the scenes is shocked to see the unceremonious, rather abusive treatment of the stage floor. And yet, although nails and stage-screws are driven into it wherever such action proves convenient—and moreover have been driven into it for whole seasons past—it is puzzling to recall that during the play there has been on the scene no evidence of the havoc wrought. The reason is simply that the stage floor proper is rarely exposed to the audience. It is covered with a huge "ground-cloth," the first thing put into place when the scene is being set. This cloth commonly has grommets around the edge; and these snap over stout "carpet-pins" driven into the stage. It is colored to befit the scene in which it is used, and frequently is painted to represent tiled pavement, parquet flooring, bare earth or some other variety that imagination will readily suggest.

In a box set the parts naturally tend to strengthen and support each other. This would be the more pronounced if all the elements mathematically corresponded; but that is far too much to expect. Flats *will* twist out of shape; stage floors *do* become uneven, and many other occasions for compromise are bound to present themselves. Thus, flats that ought to join at the sides or at the corners, simply (perhaps flatly) refuse to do so. In which circumstances the "lash-line" was invented.

High up, near the edge of one of two flats, that are to be joined, is placed a metal ring. To that ring is fastened a light, strong line. It comes down a few feet to a hook, on the edge of the adjoining flat, goes snugly around it and then descends to a hook fixed a bit lower on the first flat again. In this fashion the line staggers from side to side down to three or four feet from the stage level—the number of hooks naturally depending on the height of the scene—and there it is "tied off" to a cleat fixed on one side or the other—it doesn't particularly matter which. This method of lacing the flats together, so to speak, is amazingly successful; edges, that seem almost impossible to join evenly by any other method, thus draw smoothly into place. But should the strain be too heavy, for even the lash-line, there is available the stage-clamp, an adjustable iron instrument, pictured on a nearby page, that may be brought into action with moderate pressure of the hand, or at most a tap of a hammer, and released in the same way.

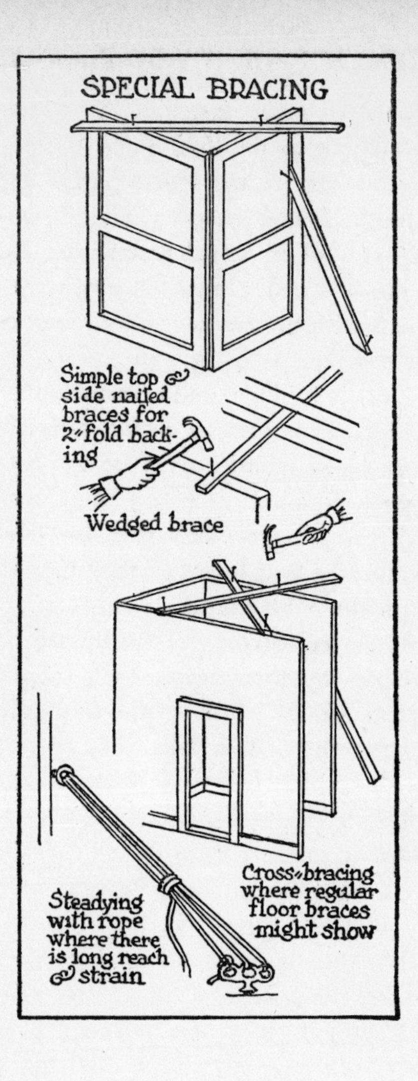
SPECIAL BRACING
Simple top & side nailed braces for 2-fold backing
Wedged brace
Steadying with rope where there is long reach & strain
Cross-bracing where regular floor braces might show

No account of stage fastenings would be complete without reference to the "pin-hinge." This is simple enough, consisting of the two separate leaves of an ordinary hinge, minus the pin. That is, a pin usually comes with it; but in actual practice on the stage the pin is frequently just a bit of heavy wire or a long, ordinary nail with the top bent over to prevent its falling through.

Although it is a hinge, and occasionally so used, the stage builder devotes it to a far different purpose. For regular hinge requirements he employs everyday hinges with fixed pins. The pin-hinge serves to connect the parts of large pieces that for one reason or another cannot be kept intact all the time. Great stairways, that seem to fill the whole stage and upon which numbers of players cavort, frequently are fabricated in a few minutes by this means, to be separated again and the parts stored in out-of-the-way corners a few moments after the curtain falls.

CHAPTER IV

UNIT CONSTRUCTION

The fewer the number of pieces, to be handled in a setting, the sooner, obviously, the scene may be assembled. For a new Broadway production this is kept in mind from the outset; and while there frequently is a salvaging of parts from failures, that have gone ignominiously to the storehouse, the whole mounting of the play begins and ends with a fairly fixed design in which there is a minimum number of units. In repertory or stock production, on the other hand, the scenic artist and his builders are obliged to consider their materials as having great adaptability that they may be used over and over again in ever-changing combinations.

That is to say, used over and over again in subsequent productions, for there is little real gain, as a rule, in making sections of scenery do double duty in the same play. If pieces may be re-used in the same play without straining to do it—and there may be cited for illustration the use of a statue in Act One in the public square, and also in Act Two as seen through the window of a house adjoining the square—the practice is legitimate enough; but generally speaking it is sufficiently economical to have each setting distinct, even when certain parts are duplicated.

Where it is intended to re-use the parts in successive

productions, however, it is manifestly wise to contrive the setting that it may be broken up easily, and to have the units of such convenient sizes and shapes that they will fit with complete flexibility into rearrangements—even into those that are as yet unknown.

Much depends upon the elaborateness of a theatre's equipment. Where money resources are ample, and storage space is not at a premium, the flats at hand come in a variety of sizes that may range in width from one foot to twenty, and in height perhaps from three to twenty-four. Flats for exterior scenes are commonly very tall, representing trees, buildings and the like; and here, therefore, is usually where the high, sixteen-, eighteen- and twenty-foot flats are to be found. If the interiors are supposed to be castle halls, of course large ones are used there, too; but modern home interiors average around twelve and fourteen feet from the stage floor. Very low flats are mainly for door and window "headers"—pieces to fill in the space from the top of the door or window to the ceiling. One of the determining factors as to extreme height is the height of the fly-floor, because, unless the flats are short enough, they cannot be stacked conveniently beneath it.

The greatest factor probably is in the sight-lines of the auditorium. Spectators in the balcony and gallery must be able to see; so if the designer falsifies a little, and makes his interior settings a bit higher than they would be in real life, he really is adding something thereby to theatregoing pleasure. Thirty or forty years ago, when stage perspectives were greatly exaggerated mainly to help spectators to see better, the ceiling of the stage room was set at a sharp tilt downward, from front to back, just as the stage floor was usually inclined toward the audience. One suspects that this may have been the way the ceiling-piece was hung in that historic first box set in 1841. An example of the ceiling-piece, made to "rake" in this manner, may be examined in a photograph of a scene in "Lord Chumly," given as an illustration in Daniel Frohman's "Memories of a Manager," and produced in the Eighties. The picture reveals two great defects of the method, one being that the ceiling is given an undue prominence, and the other that the side walls had to be cut away at an angle to accommodate it.

As to width of stock flats, it would seem that the "four" (four feet wide) is the most serviceable. A "single" (one foot wide) is as comparatively rare in stage work as it is common in the motion picture studios. The two-foot flat—now and then described as a "deuce"—is useful on the stage for making jogs, or small angles, in the wall. It is frequent for "inset" doorways, windows and so forth. The "three" has many points of merit, as has the "six," which is, however, less popular than the "eight." Wider flats are serviceable; but being unwieldy and troublesome to store, only a limited number, rarely more than half a dozen, is kept on hand. The reference now, of course, is just to stock material and not especially designed scenery.

That flats constituting a set preferably come together in a corner of some kind is self-evident. If they are "butted" in a conspicuous place, no matter how snugly the joint is made at every performance, the dividing-line shows up, while the edges become soiled from handling and rather unpleasantly increase the effect. Consequently, when the builder is obliged to contrive his settings out of a preëxisting stock of flats, with great wall areas to consider and no large pieces of which to construct them, he will combine a fitting number of small flats and keep them together with "mending battens" for the run of the play. Perhaps this is not an ideal arrangement; but workers in the theatre are accustomed to compromises of which this is an exceedingly mild example.

A builder of scenery is not, strictly speaking, a scenic artist, although it sometimes happens that the functions of both are combined in one person. What the builder is properly supposed to do is to construct the forms, upon which the scene is painted, with expert regard to stage and touring requirements. In other words, he provides the shapes and actual parts that make possible the successful realization on the stage of the artist's design. When it comes to interior settings, he can, within his own province, do nearly everything that is necessary, for modern practice there eschews the old plan of painting parts and properties in perspective on the scene. In form, at least, doors, windows, mantels, and the rest are quite real; and form is the builder's specialty. Very shallow wall-panels and light moldings, like the sort used for hanging pictures, are occasionally mere painted representations; but it is by no means impractical or difficult to build them in proper relief. Indeed, real picture-moldings, chair-rails and base or "mop" boards tend to protect the scene pieces

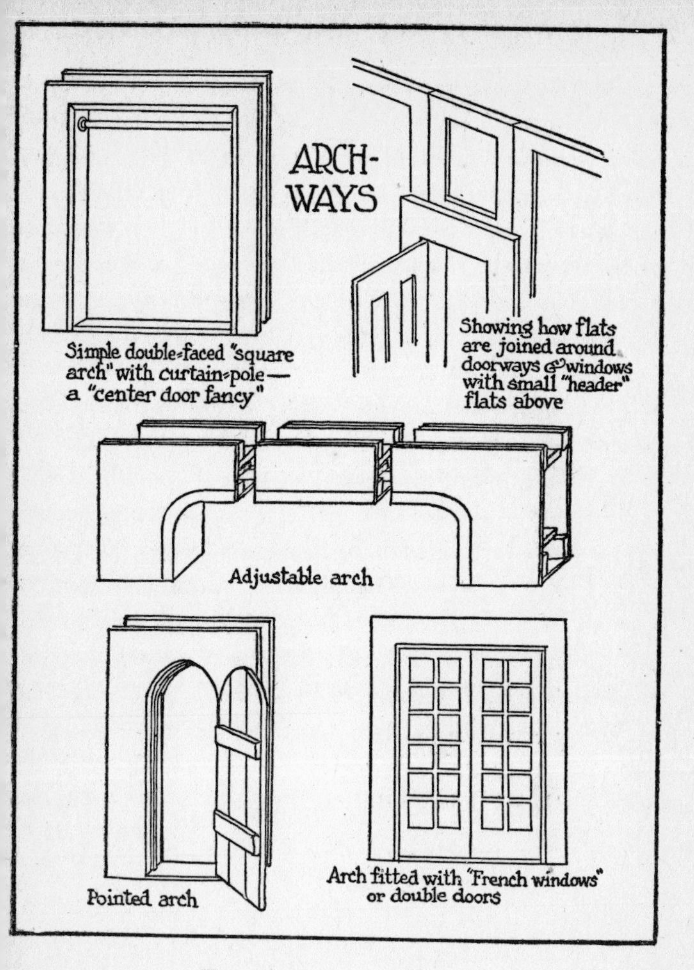

THE ARCH AS A UNIT

The small archway admits of rigid construction; wide ones tend to instability and warpage from strain. When the opening is wide, the middle portion frequently calls for reënforcement.

proper by holding them away from other surfaces against which they may be stacked.

To conceal the joints in stage walls the jog is highly useful. Edges of the flats come together at the corners just as real walls would do; and the builder is naturally careful that the cracks do not confront the spectator's direct gaze. Also, back of a jog the flats may be telescoped, affording a certain amount of "play," not only when the setting is called upon to fit larger or smaller stages, but also in putting it together upon the same stage. Variations of a few inches are easily possible at different performances in the same house.

Common sense recommends a combination of as many small parts of the setting as may be to make a single piece for quick handling. But there is no set rule about it. How far it may be done depends most upon weight and bulk involved, upon how much ought to go into the flies and how much into the wings, and on union regulations that demand clear separation of scenery, properties, and lights for handling by especial men. Generally speaking, drops, borders and large framed flats are hung in the flies; heavy pieces, like doorways, windows, mantels and staircases, are kept in the wings or at back. Nevertheless, out of the amazing ingenuity of the stage craftsman come constant exceptions to this routine. Whole house fronts, with porches, balustrades, balconies, sloping roofs, and chimneys, turn out to be all of a piece, collapsing at command like the magic, paper contraptions that the little girl with the long golden curls receives on St. Valentine's Day, and scurrying up into that dim region overhead. They are miracles, usually, of the humble pin-hinge.

When it comes to such scenic units as doors and windows, the stage builder does not regard them as do builders in outside life. To him the whole casing of the door—jambs, lintel, cap, and sill—does not belong to the wall, but is part of the unit. Window casings the same way. So, in the wings or at back of the stage, the visitor will see the door or window, already in its frame, ready to be set into the wall. The piece is in most respects as solid and substantial as a similar device would be in an actual house; only the wall is light and flimsy.

When that wall goes into place it is seen to be just an ordinary flat or combination of simple flats, with plain rectangular openings where doors and windows should be. To keep the shape of the openings and to fasten the lower edge to the stage floor, there may be light saddle-irons across their bottoms; but beyond that there is little in the appearance of the piece that has not already been described.

Doors and windows obviously must be fitted to the openings. The facings of their frames should overlap —and so conceal—the edges of the openings. If the doors and windows are double-faced—that is, reversible for use in different scenes—the facings will prevent them from being inserted; and the wall piece will have to be set upon them from above. This will be impossible, in turn, if there are saddle-irons across the bottoms of the openings. Single-faced doors and windows are easier to handle. They may be thrust through the openings after the wall is set, with no particular difficulty over the saddle-irons as long as the sills are channeled to rest upon them. The single-faced type is generally better in stage work. Reversible doors and windows are of greatest practical value in motion picture studios where there is leisure for heavy construction. A single-faced piece, moreover, is easier to prop from the rear because braces may be attached to it anywhere there without concern about marring the woodwork.

Stage doors usually are hinged to the "upstage" sides of their frames—the sides furthest from the audience—and open outward from the scene. The rule is not invariable, but it has many advantages. Hinging the door on the upstage side gives the actor unimpeded entrance and exit, and, when the door is opened, prevents the spectator from seeing much, if anything, behind the scenes. The door opening inward has corresponding disadvantages, while it frequently interferes with hidden light sources and casts embarrassing shadows.

Window and door frames being so substantial, a variety of sashes in one and of doors in the other may be changed readily. Such shifts are not made in performance, however, save in very exceptional circumstances. Each setting, once constructed, keeps its own doors and windows in their own especial frames. On the other hand, in stock and repertory theatres, it is easy to see how a great flexibility in construction is thus obtained. The same jambs, lintels and sills may accommodate, in successive, different productions,

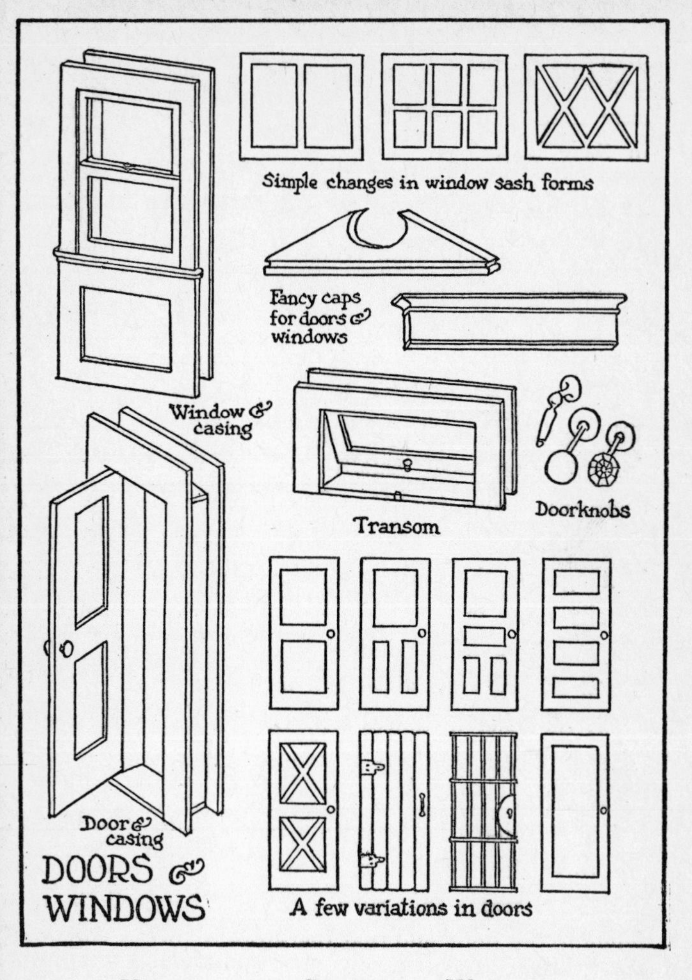

VARIATIONS IN DOORS AND WINDOWS

By making sashes and doors interchangeable in standard size frames, the scene-builder provides great flexibility in construction.

a great number of different doors and sashes, provided only that they are fairly uniform in size and match in their fastenings. Substitution means just what it would in real life. The stage door swings on common hinges and uses ordinary knobs, catches and locks, while the window-sash comes out just as one would be removed in a private dwelling for replacement of a worn-out cord.

The stage sash—if it is "practicable," which is to say, workable—has its cords and sash-weights, too, although these need not be as heavy as the house kind, for the stage sash usually has no glass in it and is therefore easier to lift. Occasionally the action requires that a window shall be smashed or that rain shall beat against the panes; and in either case, the panes usually must be provided—usually because sometimes the smashing of a window is just as effective with a sound of breaking glass and no panes at all. In virtually all other instances wherein the housewife's envy of such clean windows is aroused, there simply is no glass there.

The ordinary half-length window, one that has its sill three feet or so above the floor, is nevertheless built in a frame that runs, like the others, all the way down to the floor and that therefore is just as rigid and as easily braced. The distinction between practicable and impracticable pieces is not made so often nowadays. As modern construction goes, it is just about as easy to build a door or a window that really works as to contrive a makeshift one. A door not actually to be used probably will not be so heavily braced, and a window that is there only for appearance sake, may

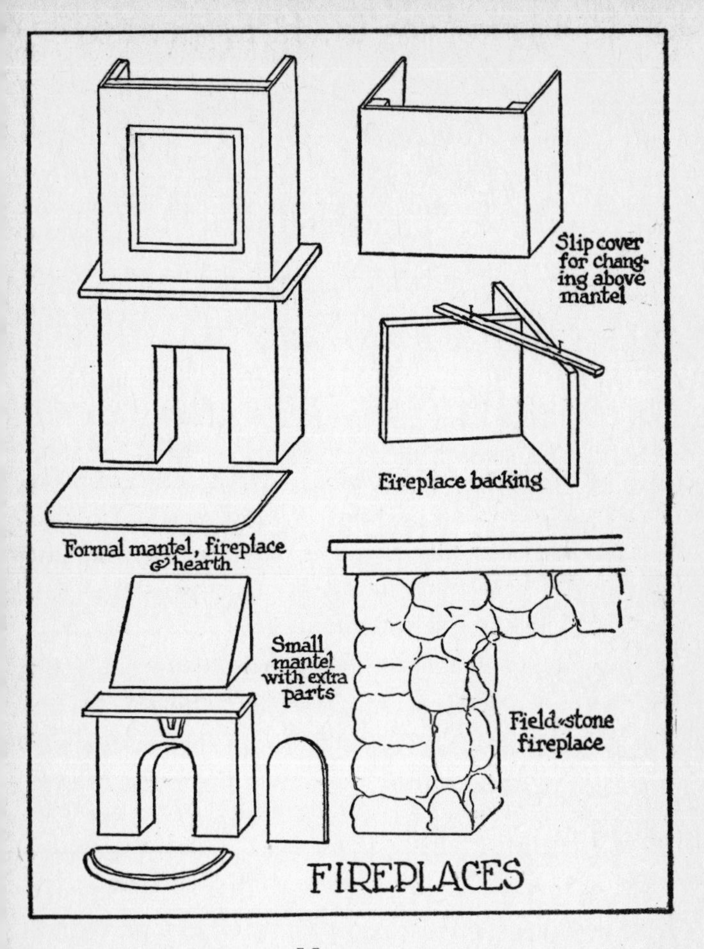

Mantels

The fireplace, conceived as a piece rising from floor to ceiling, makes a convenient masking-piece back of which the wall flats may be joined—the same advantage to be found in ordinary jogs.

have no sash-weights; but it would be no great trouble to convert either to a practical end.

The frame for a set of double doors will do equally well for a set of long "French" windows—for they really are doors of a kind. It may be used, without any windows or doors, as an open arch. It may be fitted with a curtain-pole and portières. It may be closed in below and the top made to serve as some odd-shaped, high window. It may be built up with fancy caps and moldings and supplied with a fanlight to do duty as an entrance to a Colonial mansion. In short, its service at various times is limited only by the imagination of those who command its use. What they have to consider is its basic form; and in building it in the first place, they have also to give it dimensions that will permit these possible alterations.

Doors and windows are sometimes fitted with an interesting type of brace that gives extraordinary rigidity and yet is surprisingly simple. A tall, triangular wooden frame is hinged vertically to the back of the given piece—a doorway, for example. The sill of the door is fastened to the stage floor with a couple of stage-screws. The triangular brace is then swung outward; and its thrust being opposed to that of the screws, the door is virtually wedged into position.

But whatever goes into the openings of the wall, in a stage scene, they remain openings still. Measures must be taken to limit the spectator's view through them. Here is where "backings" prove useful. A backing sometimes is a large drop, especially when it represents things seen simultaneously through several windows or doors in the same plane—a landscape, perhaps, or hallways and other rooms in an interior. The common backing, however, is the two-fold flat. Opened at an angle it supports itself on the stage floor, like a screen, and is fixed there easily with a stage-brace.

CHAPTER V

ELEVATIONS

THE scenic architect, being presumably a person of imagination who knows but is not dominated by stage limitations, does not stop by conceiving a scene with variable top and sides; he also debates the possibility of an uneven ground. Nor does he confine himself to elevations; he thinks of depressions as well—and the stage floor, as it happens, is usually prepared to meet demands for either or both. By lifting a panel or two out of the stage floor, there is room for a stairway, for example, going down, let us say, from a second story scene to the first story. The only extensive building demanded in this case is that the carpenter shall provide some six or seven feet below the stage—far enough down to allow head-room for an exit—a landing platform, and a ladder if the cellar floor is much lower.

A useful platform to have below the stage is a trap. Of course, that device is intended primarily to lift players, with magical effect, up through the stage floor; but it may be fixed at any height on the way and used merely for a landing. Its construction, shown in an accompanying sketch, involves a counterweighted platform traveling vertically in a frame, its speed controlled by a stagehand nearby at a rope with a bight in it. In its most elaborate form the trap is made au-

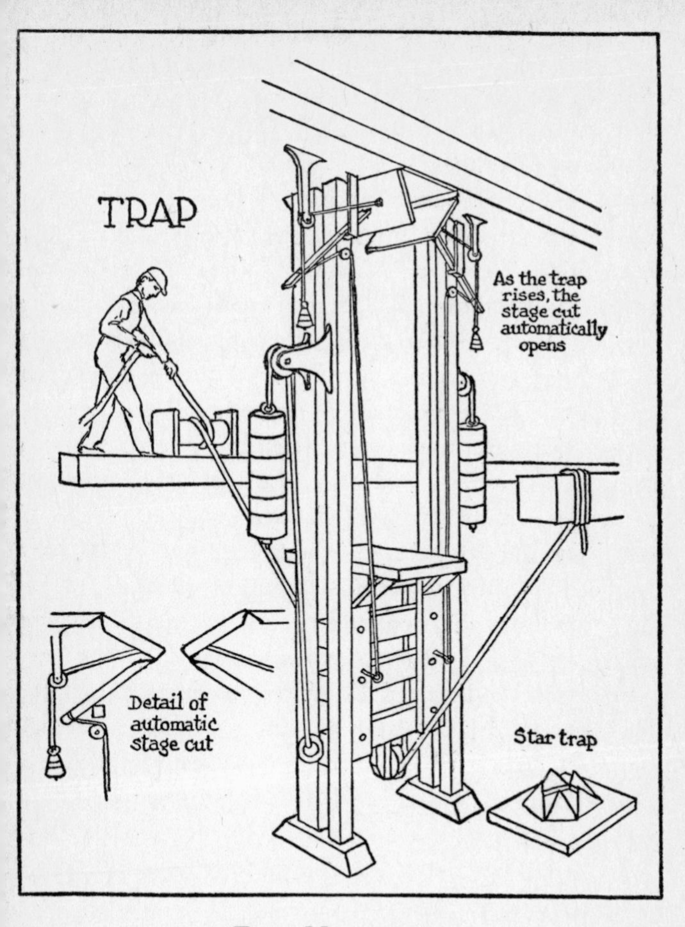

TRAP MACHINERY

All traps are not as elaborate as this, but, in one form or another every well-made trap embodies these features—a counterweighted platform rising in a groove and an automatic stage opening. Without the latter, a player lifted on the platform might sustain injury.

tomatically to open the stage floor above it as it ascends, closing it again as it comes down. Into the opening, sometimes, is fitted a cover that lifts in points when a player is shot upward through it, closing immediately thereafter by the force of elastic bands underneath. This type of cover is known as the star trap. Another kind is a screen made of stiff bristles meeting in the center, fitting the player's body snugly as he comes through, and, of course, closing after him.

A level above the stage is something more complicated. Engineers, who have tried to bring to ordinary stage construction what they consider more scientific principles, frequently have devised elaborate means to raise (or lower) parts of the stage; but it has been found in practice that the size and position of one of these arbitrary divisions are not always convenient for given settings. In the Asphaleia system the stage level was broken and varied by hydraulic plungers; in the plan devised much later by the celebrated English architect, Edwin O. Sachs, and still used in the Royal Opera House, Covent Garden, London, the stage floor was divided into a succession of transverse "bridges" operated up or down by counterweights and electric motors in combination.

Such equipment is no doubt very much worth while in houses where spectacular productions involving huge casts are the rule, and where a platform, above or below, not only must be stout enough to sustain the weight of fifty or more persons, but may also have to move with them on it. In smaller theatres the installation of such elaborate and costly equipment is impractical.

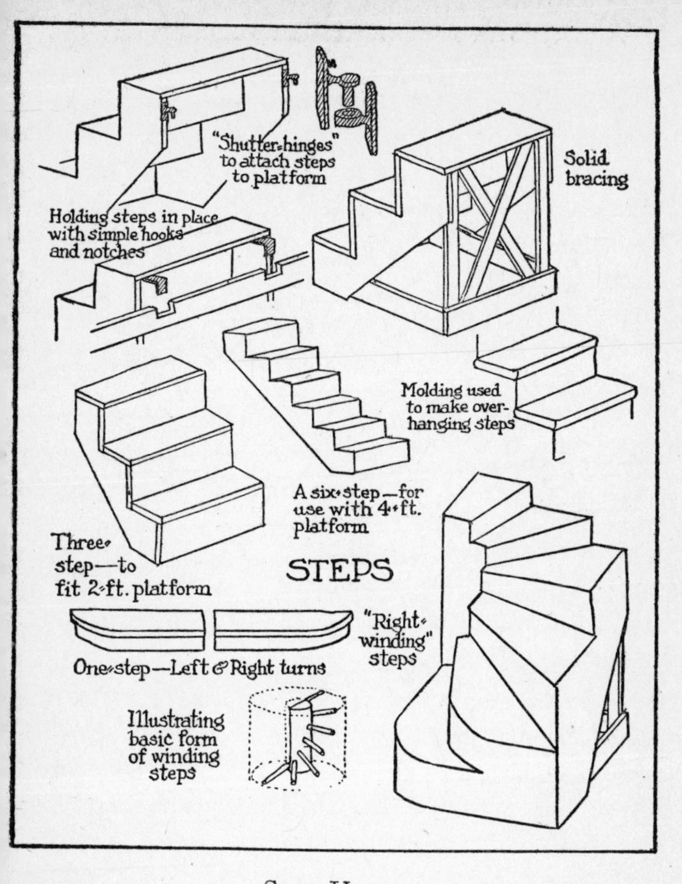

Step Units

The unit system of building saves much labor backstage, for, in accordance with it, each piece may be used over and over again in successive productions. Steps in the above illustration are designed for use in various combinations for narrow flights or broad staircases of different heights. They are made to correspond with the platforms shown in the frontispiece.

Smaller stages succeed very well with more modest platforms. These "parallels," as they are called, are exceedingly simple in construction, and, when not in use, can be stored away as easily as a two-fold flat. A sketch in the frontispiece shows clearly how they are made, the four sides hinged that the piece may be collapsed like the proverbial house of cards. When it is opened, a fitted top is placed over it much as a ceiling-piece is made to complete the box set. Fastened there, it makes the platform rigid enough for all practical purposes. To hold the whole piece in position, to keep it from sliding around the stage or tipping over with extraordinary weight on one side, the ever-ready stage-brace is requisitioned, nails are driven through the legs into the stage floor, or stage-screws are set through simple fixtures made to accommodate them.

The top of the parallels need not be in line with the floor. As indicated in the sketch, the device may be used just as well for an incline, or "run"; and it may be that a stage builder will conceive an even more complicated shape to meet the especial needs of some odd setting.

As platforms may be joined, as readily as flats, there is no especial advantage in having very large ones. Probably the most serviceable all-around sizes are parallels that make platforms respectively eight and sixteen feet long and four feet wide. In height the most convenient sizes probably are two feet and four feet, this because sets of steps, to be used with them, usually run eight inches to the riser—three steps making the two feet, and six, of course, the four. For greater

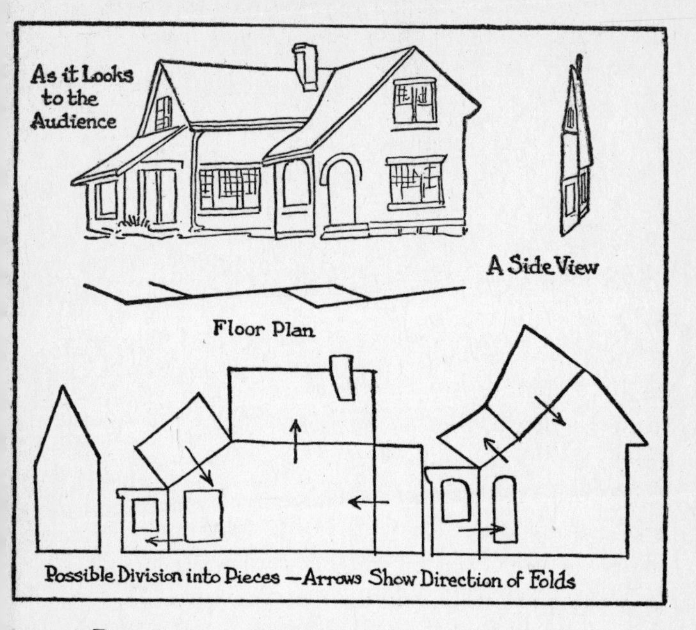

BUILDING IN FORESHORTENED PERSPECTIVE

In a shallow space of four or five feet from front to back this entire cottage, with practicable doors, windows and porches and real sloping roofs, may be shown effectively without encroachment on the acting zone.

height than four feet, two or more platforms may be mounted, one atop the other, and held there with mending battens or any other reasonable devices. A moment's reflection will show that, even in such combination, they still may be collapsed.

Steps to reach the platforms from the stage level are separately built, and, save in certain trick work, are fixed in construction. Collapsible parts there, ordinarily, might result in serious injury to the players. An added advantage in fixed forms is that the steps then may be given individuality. They may thus be made to show irregular design, the sag of years of wear, or the uneven tipping of ancient stone blocks. Four feet is the convenient width, enabling the scene-builder to set the steps neatly at the end of the parallels, or to join two or more staircases completely to front the eight or sixteen-foot platforms.

This matter of keeping scenic equipment as compact as possible is a vital one. Scenery is fundamentally a background for the action of the play; and it ought to leave ample space for the players. The acting zone must not be cluttered with sprawling platforms or other cumbrous pieces unless such condition is justified by fairly constant use—especially true in musical comedy productions where there is much dancing. This fact the experienced scene-builder knows well; and he tries in every reasonable way to meet the demand. One of his most successful solutions of the difficulty lies in what any artist calls foreshortening. That is, the spectator, from his fixed point of view, can best judge distances in the vertical plane; he cannot accurately detect distances the other way, from front to back. Therefore the scene-builder shortens distances in the last-named horizontal plane, materially increasing stage space for the actor. He falsifies his perspective, but works no real harm thereby to the scenic effect. It is astonishing how far this method may be carried without destroying the illusion. A cottage, perhaps, may be shown at an angle with two whole sides visible, doors and windows in actual use; and yet the whole device will occupy a stage depth of less than six feet. Steps are somewhat of an exception. The scene-builder may

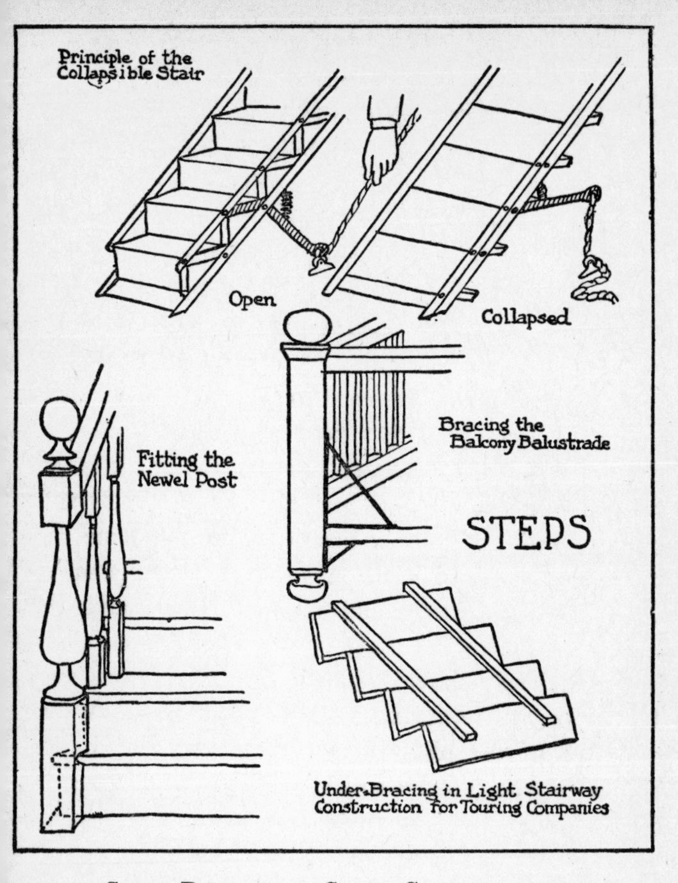

Some Details of Stair Construction

Trick steps, used now and then in native musical farces and commonly in foreign pantomimes, are made in many ways of which the above has been chosen as representative. The sketches of balustrade fittings are of particular importance in the unit system of building which requires that balustrades shall be detachable. In ordinary construction the balustrade is permanently fixed to the steps.

avoid broad ones, but he must provide treads that will give the actor full, firm foothold.

Balustrades are separately built, being made fast to the stairways as required. How they are attached depends altogether upon the ingenuity of the builder. Sometimes an iron brace pulls up part way out of the staircase and is fastened, with wing-nuts on bolts, to the balustrade. But however the joint is made, the balustrade should be rigid.

The steps may be fastened to the platform to which they give access, but they need not necessarily be. A solidly built flight of stairs, portable though it is, still has considerable weight; and this frequently is sufficient to keep the unit in position. At the same time there are occasions when a stairway is the zone of violent physical action; and Safety First demands that it may not be rocked away or wrenched loose. As to how a stairway should be made secure, opinions vary. It may be fitted with simple hooks that will lock over the edge of the platform; or there may be shutter-hinges on the pin-and-socket principle. Objectors to these methods are sometimes just opposed to any sort of projecting hook that may punch a hole in scenery; and their substitute way of doing it may be to nail the stair fast, or to lash it from underneath, for both stairs and platforms are open in that part.

It is not enough, in most cases, just to have a platform for the stairs to lead to; the actor who ascends to the top must have something on which to stand when he goes off through the upper door. Sometimes, therefore, the platform juts through the wall for his convenience. At other times a second platform is erected there. In either case, if the actor is to remain off the scene following his exit, he must not be marooned on this outside height until the curtain descends. On the offstage side, therefore, he finds a ladder by which he descends again to the stage level. But ordinary ladders are not ideally adapted to the use of ladies. If the player chances to be an actress, she is entitled to something more befitting her dignity. There is also risk of soiling and tearing costumes in using ladders. Moreover, falling from a ladder may shake the whole scene and ruin the play.

In all events, a well-run stage provides for such needs, affording commonly what is a sort of step-ladder fitted with a hand-rail. With the aid of this the player descends in moderate comfort. However, should a stagehand be questioned as to the purpose of such contrivances, he probably will say that they are primarily for the stage crew itself to climb to places otherwise difficult of access.

In truth, every management that denies comfortable offstage stairways does not deserve to be called stingy or ill-natured. Comfortable stairways take up valuable room offstage as well as they do in the acting zone. The ordinary vertical ladder occupies almost minimum space, the only device that goes it one better being the fireman's pole down which he slides from his bunk when an alarm comes in. This pole is a stage device, too, especially in large spectacles where players must descend quickly from some very high places.

Regular step-ladders also have plenty of uses backstage—usually appearing in three sizes, probably five feet, six or seven feet and ten. For moderate heights an ordinary kitchen chair serves. Where there is storage room, it is well for a stage to have three or four rough platforms for exclusive use behind the scenes. Platforms of this kind are not collapsible, but are permanently braced. They range in height, as a rule, from about six feet to eight or ten. The lower ones are commonly about four by six, and fairly heavy in construction. These may be used as part of the scene, to hold heavy scene pieces that require such elevation, or perhaps to sustain a battery of special lights. These, of course, are mere routine uses. Like all other backstage paraphernalia, they are pressed into any kind of work that they can be made to do. They are shifted constantly. To move them they are occasionally fitted with rubber-tired ball-bearing casters that may be blocked or locked by a patent arrangement when the platform comes to rest; but more often they are just lifted bodily from place to place by a couple of husky lads.

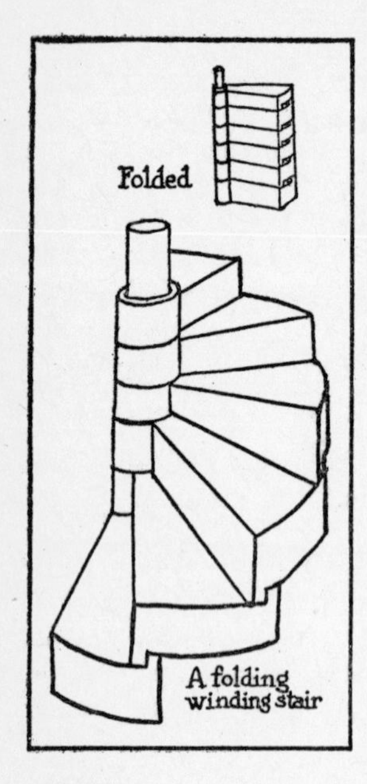

The regulation light-stand is a wooden platform from eight to ten feet high—fifteen or eighteen in the houses where spectacular productions obtain—only about two by three feet at top, and not much larger at bottom. The reason for this slender form is that portable lights usually have to go in narrow places, between the side wall of the scene and the backing for the windows or doors, in the first entrances close to the proscenium arch, or in positions still more difficult. The height is gauged that the lamp used may be able to overlook an ordinary flat, used as a backing, and "spot" a player on the scene. At the top of the stand, a little to one side of the middle, a stout iron pipe protrudes about three feet. Underneath, it goes on down into the body of the stand where it is securely braced. This pipe is an anchor, so to speak, to hold the lamp when that is put into position atop the stand. The pipe is off-center, partly that when the light is inclined, as it usually is, it will not overturn the stand. Also, this gives the operator a footing. Pictures of light-stands are given on page 109.

A ladder, provided as part of the stand, helps to reenforce it. The usual light mounted in this fashion, is the full-size "spot." It is an exceedingly weighty affair; and as the electrician who attends it is not selected for his slightness of build, it may readily be imagined that reënforcement of the narrow tower is a serious problem. One method is "toeing" nails into the floor through the supporting legs; others include the stage-brace with its accompanying stage-screws; sometimes the bottom is weighted, and an interesting form carries one corner of the stand out at an angle to make the whole thing a sort of tripod. Although the stand is used, as a rule, in narrow quarters, there usually is at least one open space through which the odd leg may be thrust and made fast to the floor.

In the case of the light-stand, as in that of the lower,

utility platform earlier mentioned, casters are sometimes used; but here again the common form of locomotion is for stagehands to lift it up and carry it. From this chance remark about "utility" platforms it must not be gathered that the light-stand is not used also for many alien purposes. It may be pressed into service for numerous effects, among which may be remarked that of an actor who seems to the audience in front to be seated comfortably in an upper window of a fine house.

Now and then the stage builder is called upon to provide an elevation with an open space beneath it. The actor must seem, perhaps, to be standing on a bridge. Scenic construction for this must be light for transportation, and it must be strong. An obvious solution is to put a few planks from one fixed platform to another, one platform hidden back of each pier of the pretended arch. If the reach is too long for single planks, cables may be stretched over the platforms on turnbuckles—much as they set a foothold for the "tight-rope" dancer in vaudeville—and a runway is put over that. If the scene is a wide balcony seen in profile, and for which there can be a supporting platform at only one side, the other end of the runway is supported by stout lines from the gridiron. The gridiron always has place for special pulley-blocks to be attached where necessary.

A touring company cannot always count on finding these fixed platforms in theatres visited. In fact, it may be doubted that any theatrical traveler ever does expect them; and as platforms of this sort cannot conveniently be carried, the company has a light form of

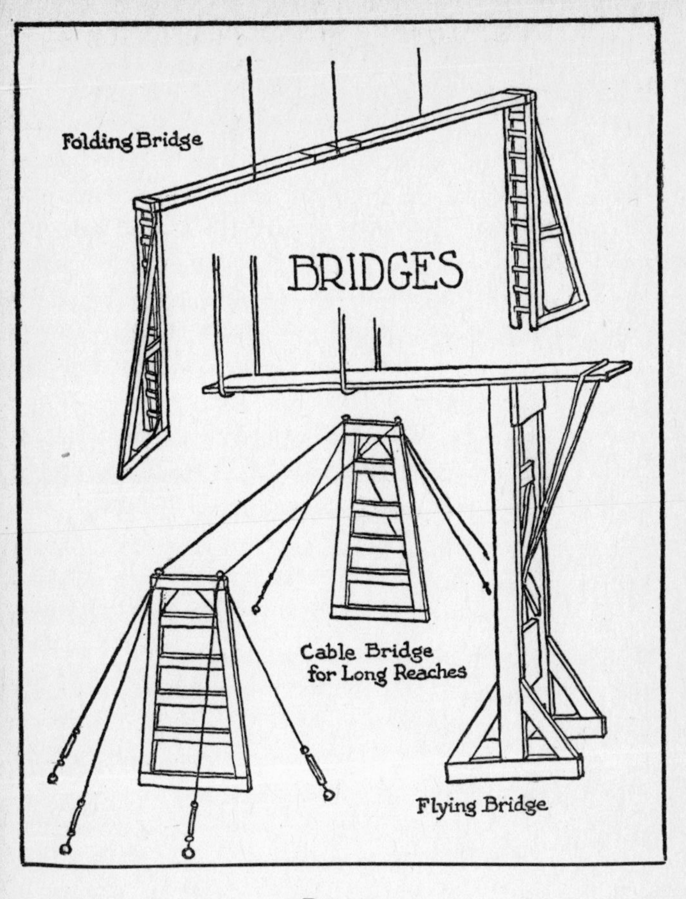

Bridges

In the frontispiece .. indicated a bridge that travels back and forth on rails on a level with the fly-gallery floor; but this, as a part of permanent stage equipment, is uncommon. Portable forms, of which those in this illustration are typical, usually serve the same end.

bridge that is adaptable to many purposes. Here is the way it is built: The support at each end of the bridge is a two-fold, consisting of a ladder and a triangular brace of equal height, hinged together. These parts are opened at an angle and braced in the usual manner to the stage floor. The runway, that is to stretch between them, is hinged and folded perhaps as many as three times. It is opened out and attached at due intervals to a set of lines from the gridiron which bears much of the weight. The ends are slipped over the aforesaid supports from below, and the bridge is complete. The structure is commonly strong enough to support fifteen or twenty persons at one time.

CHAPTER VI

IRREGULAR PIECES

Building pieces "in the round," which is to say in such complete form that they may be viewed successfully from any angle, has many conveniences. They may be painted without difficult considerations of perspective, and they may be re-used for subsequent productions in varied positions on the stage. But, although these points of merit are undeniable, it is not always easy for the inexpert stage builder to realize them in practice. The flat surfaces he can master; but curved ones present such highly technical problems that they frighten him off.

The secret of building a curved surface—if secret there be—is mainly in making the frame that holds it. The actual surface is comparatively simple to provide these days. It consists, as a rule, of just one of the many patent wall-boards procurable at any lumber-yard. Its use is almost as varied, on a large scale, as ordinary paper is in a kindergarten. It cannot be folded; but it may be cut—and hammer and nails serve the same end there as paste in the hands of the children. Cubes and cylinders and many other geometrical forms, are thus produced by nearly identical methods.

Wall-board, in the present uses, behaves like a very heavy cardboard. There is a natural spring to it. Fasten a strip of it at either end so that it bulges in the middle, and the board will make a graceful bow between the two points. Consequently, if the supporting frame merely provides braces every foot or so along the desired arc, this board will complete the curve across the open spaces. That is how they make an archway in stage work. The span consists of a series of wooden struts between the back and front, with a bend of wall-board nailed over them.

A bay-window or an alcove is made in the same manner, save that if the alcove has a coved ceiling it will require a little special figuring and cutting. A concavity like this involves not merely one curve but several, for it is, with modifications, perhaps, a quarter-sphere. There is no more graphic illustration of the making of a sphere, in whole or in part, than a peeled orange. Observing that popular fruit in this naked condition, one may notice that the back of each segment is ovate; that is, it consists of two reversed curves coming together at top and bottom as points. The sphere comprises a given number of these set side by side in a ring with their upper and lower points drawn together. The stage sphere—or hemisphere, or quarter-sphere or any other fraction, thereof—is usually made by this same principle. The ovate shapes, called gores, are cut out of flat pieces of wall-board and bent to cover a rounded framework. It is the same scheme employed by geographers to make terrestrial globes. The wall-board may be cut with a saw, or "scored" with a sharp knife, and "broken."

In the construction of a symmetrical form, like a globe, the stage builder realizes that, as the parts duplicate each other, all he has to plan is one part.

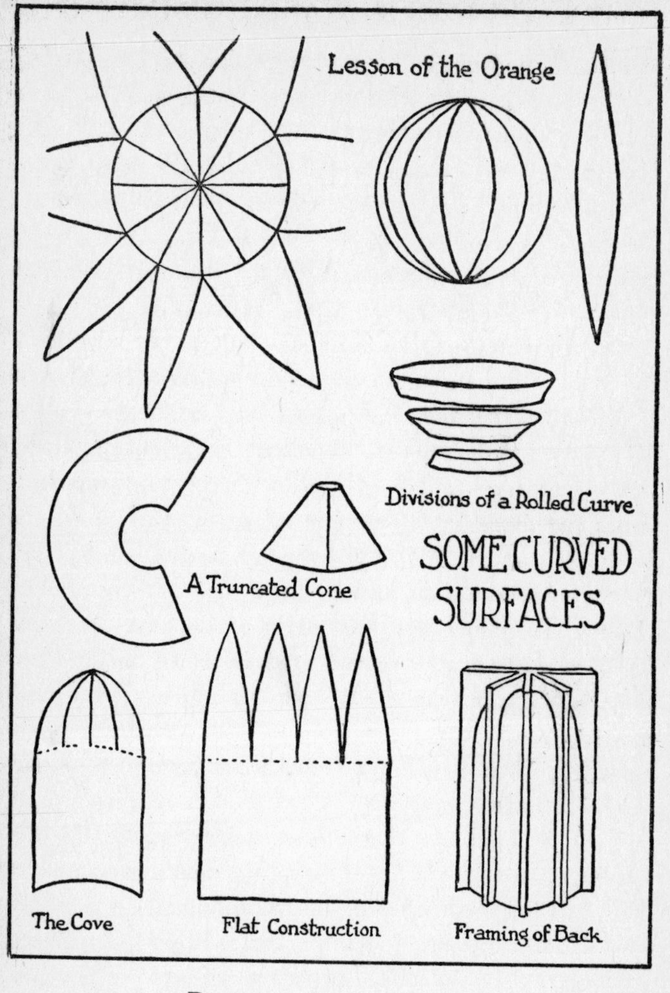

ROUNDED SCENE-PIECES

Even a casual working knowledge of geometrical forms is of great assistance in building cones, spheres and their varieties.

Having done that, he has a pattern for the rest. With a single gore in hand, therefore, the others are easy to make. The supporting frame is just a series of ribs, braced as necessary, corresponding with the lines where the gores join, and to which the gores may be nailed. To find the required number of gores (as also of ribs in the frame) the circumference of the sphere is divided into an equal number of parts. The more parts, the smoother the curve of the finished surface. Length of the gore is not the diameter of the sphere—for that is the distance between the points only after they have been bent into place—but one-half the circumference, the circumference being roughly three and one-half times the diameter. The side curves of the gore may be made very readily by any high-school student of geometry who knows how to draw an arc through any three given points. In fact, every student of geometry has learned to reduce complicated forms in one, two or three dimensions to their simplest aspects; and the builder puzzled over problems of that nature will do well, therefore, to call upon such a mathematical person for assistance.

Strictly speaking, the builder ought to know some geometry for himself, for he is expected, at the very outset of his work, to plan, as accurately as an architect would make his specifications for a house, the pieces that will make the scenic artist's original sketches and models practicable. One need not be a mathematical wizard to know the ordinary helpfulness of compasses, rules, triangles, and T-squares. Some knowledge of them will be useful. The designer is not always careful about details of scale. More often than not the builder receives from him only a rough sketch on the back of an envelope and is told to make it come true.

Forms, as the scene-builder (like the geometrician) sees them, are therefore generally compounds of simpler shapes; and when he reproduces or creates them, he does so in units, although he may fasten those units permanently together before his work is complete. For single planes he thinks principally in terms of circles, squares and triangles, and, for solid forms bounded by planes, his basic conceptions involve cubes, cylinders, cones, pyramids, spheres and their varieties. Knowing best how to construct these elementary forms, he may modify their lines easily to conform with their illusory purposes. What is supposed to be a solid mound of earth may be built in the main as a truncated cone or pyramid with irregularities added afterward. A lighthouse on a rock may consist for him of at least three parts, a prism for the rock, a cylinder for the tower and a cone for the roof. But then, any art student conceives his drawing in virtually the same way with his "blocking-in" lines.

After the simple, curved archway, the most-used rounded surfaces to be fitted into a unit system of construction, are columns. Now, of course, there are such things as square columns, and they are useful items to have; but the round column is especially valuable when so much of the rest of the scene is constituted by straight lines and needs relief. A round stage column (and a square one, too) is thought of, in the approved architectural way, as base, shaft and capital, these being separate pieces. The shaft, or column proper, is the most difficult to build, the laborious part of that being the frame around which wall-board is rolled and nailed fast. An accompanying picture shows the construction of this frame sufficiently well to dispense with a verbal description of it.

For ordinary purposes a stage column is of the same size top and bottom; but for very sound reasons of architectural beauty—which is to say, artistic effect—the usual real-life column is made to taper from its base to a slightly smaller top. The scene-builder generally observes this rule only in the tall columns where such tapering is marked. In small ones the parallel sides make it immaterial which end the column stands upon, and enables transposed capital and base to fit equally well. In cutting the wall-board, to be wrapped around the frame of the attenuated column, the builder must bear in mind that he now is making not a cylinder but a truncated cone, and must lay out the dimensions of his wall-board accordingly.

The simplest cap and base for a small vertical column are interchangeable. Each consists merely of a square board or block with a round molding upon it to make a ring into which the column fits. The round molding is made from a straight wooden one that is "scored," or sawed about two-thirds through, at intervals of about half an inch throughout its length, the result being that it may be bent easily to fit the desired marks. The saw-cuts may be filled with putty; but as a rule the builder leaves them as they are, for such details do not usually "show up" to the audience. Sometimes the base is fastened permanently to the column. More often it is not fastened, because the stagehand who assembles the

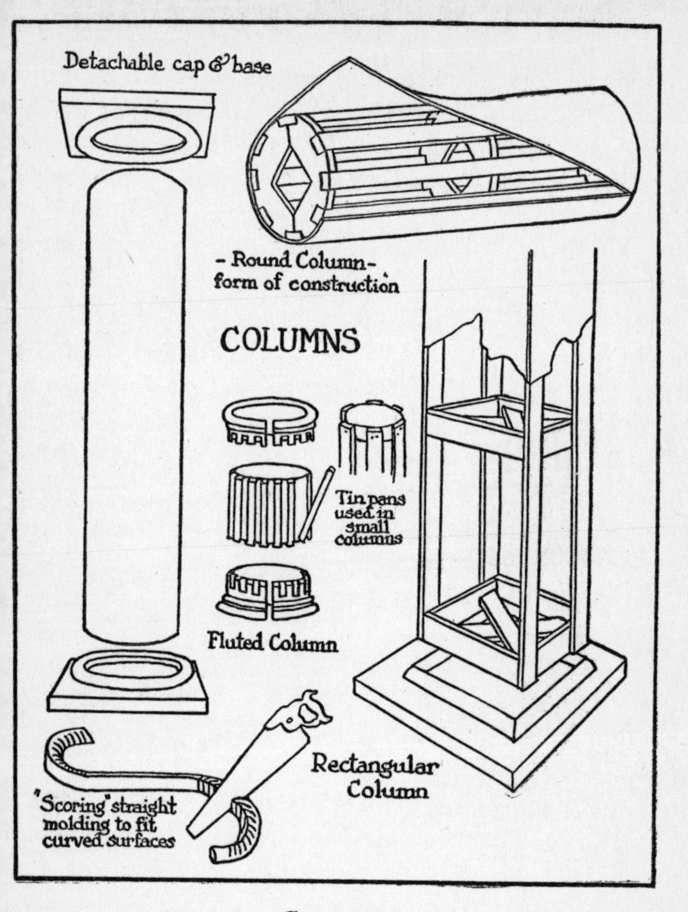

COLUMNS

The round column at left is of the same diameter top and bottom, and therefore is not in accord with strict canons of architecture. However, the fact is of great convenience in scene-building. Swelling and tapering columns are not impossible, but demand more intricate construction and more careful handling.

scene then has an extra opportunity to adjust it. The cap probably will be fastened to the piece that makes the whole top of the pediment or wall, or whatever it is that the column is supposed to support, the column being thrust into place beneath it. In stage work what appears to support heavy parts of the scene probably does not do so at all, a fact already shown in descriptions of stage walls and doors.

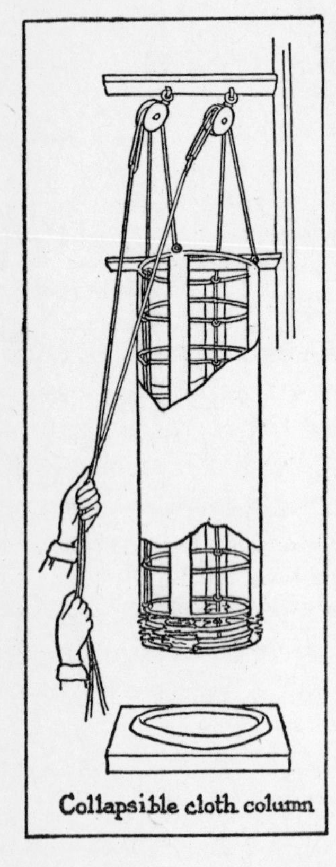
Collapsible cloth column

Coming to the use of fancy capitals, like the Corinthian, Byzantine, and Gothic, the builder's resources, as heretofore described, are insufficient. He is entering the realm of sculpture. Nevertheless, he need not be wholly daunted provided he can find some one who can model sufficiently well to copy the established designs.

The design carved at top of a column almost invariably repeats itself a minimum of four times around the capital, once for each "corner." This means that the modeler need only work out one corner, because, by a simple process at once to be detailed, it may be duplicated in as many corners and as many capitals as may be needed.

Probably the builder has begun by making a light framework for the capital, a simple base to hold the ornament. The artist applies modeling clay to one complete corner—or to as large a section as is demanded by the "repeat" of the design—and shapes it to the final form. A heavy plaster cast is then made of the artist's handiwork, giving an impression in intaglio. When dry and firm, this is thoroughly brushed or sprayed with shellac; and the mold or matrix being "set" in its own due time, it is well oiled to receive, without sticking, the substance from which duplicates are to be produced.

The best substance is *carton-pierre,* a *papier-mâché.* As the latter implies, this consists mainly of mashed or macerated paper. Sometimes the builder is able to purchase a quantity of wood or rag pulp from a neighboring paper mill; but more often he is obliged to manufacture it for himself. He has many ways of doing this; but a method as good as any is to pound a lot of soaked newspapers with mortar and pestle until they are well shredded. The addition of a quantity of melted glue size, some bole, and a little chalk, converts the mass into a stiff but workable paste. This, introduced into the mold, is pressed carefully into all the depressions and then permitted to dry a little. Finally it is taken out, at which time it is seen to have the form of the original clay model. The process is, of course, repeated for all the corners.

Assembling the corners, when they are well dried, is a comparatively simple matter. *Papier-mâché* may be glued and it may also be nailed, which is a common way of mounting it on the frame. It is very light and it is well-nigh indestructible. In any reasonable circumstances it will not shrink and it will not warp, and obviously, it may be painted. But, while *papier-mâché* is all very well for the production of ornament, there are many other likely purposes for which it is complicated and expensive. When large areas of the stage must be modeled up as hillsides, hummocks, and rocks, it is more practicable to use another means.

The stage scene involving what is called simply "built-up ground," starts with a floor-cloth as most other settings do. In this case the cloth is usually painted a grass green or a sandy "ground" color, or it may be divided up into parts, perhaps a "path" in one place, the tiles of a courtyard in another and so on, depending, naturally, on what the setting as a whole is intended to represent. Judiciously placed about the floor to cover cracks or sprawling cables, or perhaps just to help out the general illusion of reality, may be small "grass mats." These are patches of imitation greensward made of bunches of tough dried grass sewed together with carpet-thread to form rugs, all fireproofed and dyed. Some of these rugs are made large enough to cover the entire stage; but that sort is costly and cumbersome.

Here and there, too, will be found stage "rocks," very satisfactorily made of workshop odds and ends, which is to say, mainly out of old boxes so cut down that they rest on the stage floor at queer, futuristic angles, the weathered contours provided by whimsical twists and folds of odd bits of canvas tacked into

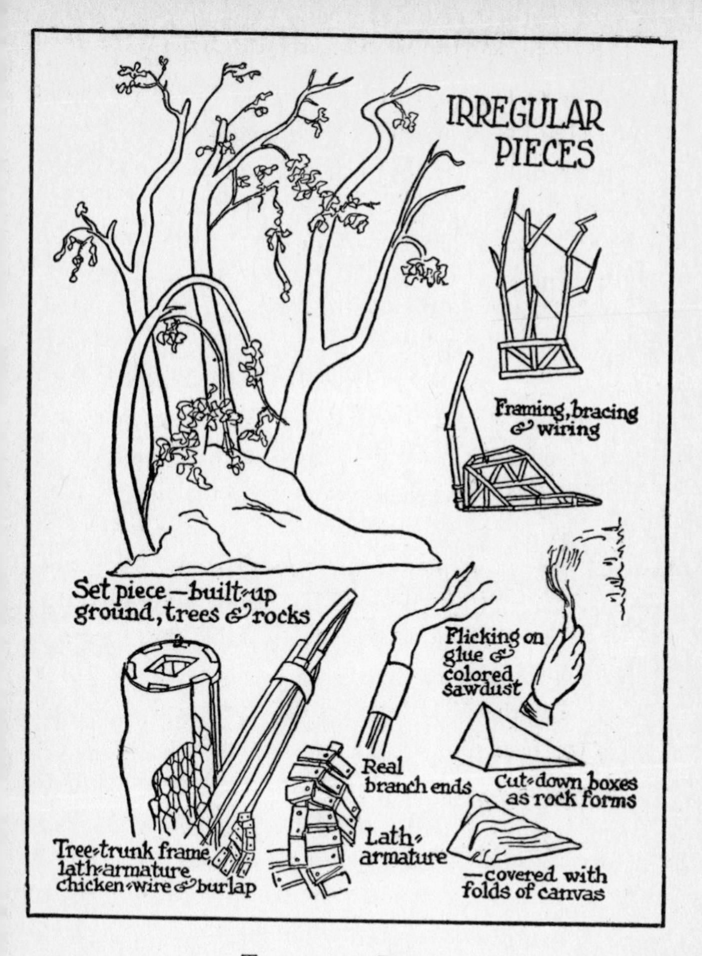

TREES AND ROCKS

There is more difference of method here than in any other building phase. Each problem is a new one to test ingenuity. But this is the approved way to do these particular things. The subject is discussed further in Chapter VII.

place. As to that part of the floor of the scene representing tiles, as aforesaid, if the conscientious builder is not content to have them painted on the cloth, he may make very interesting and effective ones by cutting them out of wall-board and mounting them on convenient panels of the same. These panels, joined in place and lightly tacked to the floor, will bear close inspection.

Coming to greater unevenness of floor, the builder begins to use "runs," or inclines, with the imitation surface overlaid. He must always think, however, of portability and convenience in storing the pieces when not in use. Consequently, a broad hillside may consist of three or four separate runs joined. Pieces of this sort are rarely stock affairs, being built to order for given productions. For this reason they are not wholly made, as a rule, to bear heavy weights. If a pathway up the hillside must be "practicable," must sustain the hero and heroine as they walk together out into the sunset, that portion must be braced and reenforced. On the other hand, those portions that are needed only to support bunches of violets and bits of heather, need no such solid construction, with consequent gain in lightness for handling.

These lighter places are built in an interesting and peculiar way. The basic frame is made in the general nature of a run, with, of course, particular bracings and modifications of form. The superficial differences of form are indicated roughly, atop this frame, by smaller constructions of light wood; and over the whole are then fastened strips of "chicken" or meshed wire, cut and bent as necessary to make the contours of the "ground." Over this wire, in turn, are tacked pieces of canvas, or burlap, completing the surface as far as the builder is concerned. Artificial flowers and moss are put into place later.

Then there are trees. A stage tree-trunk, to be shown solidly "in the round," has for its basic construction a frame like that of the round column. From this are built out the heavier "branches"; and if these branches are especially heavy, they may be braced with cross-wires, the wires to be masked by smaller branches or details of foliage. For ends real branches may be used, fastened on with metal sleeves. Boles and other pronounced excrescences are built up with bits of lath, with the usual meshed wire over that, and over that, again, twists of canvas or burlap to imitate the bark.

Hedges—especially of the formal "boxed" order—are made of light frames covered with meshed wire to which is sewn green velvet. The nap of the velvet is glued down in spots, each spot about the size of a man's thumb, so that the whole has a mottled appearance that, at distance, admirably counterfeits the actual surface. An untrimmed hedge, or top of a boxwood tree, is sometimes made of a frame covered with heavy green denim which acts as a backing for sprays of artificial leaves fastened to it.

Fancy iron gates and grill-work are usually just pieces of wall-board cut out with a jig-saw and braced from the rear. Straight iron bars are made quite obviously of wood. Loose bricks in a wall are just suitable pieces sliced from an ordinary "two-by-four," while if a brick is to be thrown to hit somebody, it is made of a cloth form filled with cotton, or other stuffing such as would normally be used in a sofa-cushion, the sound of the impact being simulated by a separate effect offstage.

CHAPTER VII

THE PAINT FRAME

A PAINT FRAME is a very large, flat, wooden frame, thoroughly braced, and so suspended that it may be raised and lowered bodily and stopped at any point. Upon this frame is fastened the drop that is to be painted. In fact, flats are fastened to it, too, for the same purpose.

It is raised and lowered, for the convenience of the painter, so that he may reach every part. This means that it should have a space, in which to move vertically, of approximately twice its own height. In the average theatre the only place that is so lofty is the stage itself; and consequently the painter sometimes does his work there. This has a great added advantage in that he can view his work under the stage lights whenever he wants to. He takes his position on a narrow gangway, that crosses from one side to the other, at about the level of the first fly-galleries, the paint frame moving up and down beside it like an ordinary drop. This gangway is called the "paint bridge." Like the paint frame the paint bridge frequently gives its name to the whole realm of the scene-painter, just as the word stage is made to apply also to the entire world behind the scenes.

Nowadays the law tends to discourage all scene-painting on the stage because of fire hazards. The scene pieces not yet fireproofed constitute one risk; but most serious of all is the little stove on which the painter melts his glue size. More than one stage fire has resulted from that single cause. The menace may be understood more clearly when it is explained that in many of the stock theatres the scene-painter labors up in the flies even during performance on the stage below. It is serious enough to have a fire in an empty theatre; but a blaze with an audience present is worse.

The ideal arrangement is to have the paint frame in a place altogether to itself and just for paint purposes. However, what precisely constitutes an ideal scheme depends largely upon the artist's point of view. In Latin countries scenery is painted flat on the floor, the artist walking over the surface while he works with long-handled brushes; in England and in America, the common practice is to hang a drop vertically and either to move the drop up and down before the artist or move the artist up and down before the drop. Moving the artist means, of course, that the roof of the *atelier* need not be nearly as high as in the case of moving the drop, although sometimes an ingenious idea, of slitting the floor and lowering the drop into the cellar, makes a fairly low roof possible even for the adjustable frame plan. In all events, the English way is far more economical of floor space than the French or Italian.

To be able to see the whole drop at one time is a distinct advantage; so probably the best arrangement, compromising with medium roofs, is for the artist to do most of the moving. If the drops he paints are very large, he ought to have an adjustable scaffold. If they are not higher than eighteen or twenty feet, a

THE SMALL PAINT FRAME

pair of stout step-ladders, with a couple of planks across, will serve very well. Even with a low studio roof it is almost always possible to raise or lower the paint frame three or four feet; and this easily brings the top of the average drop within reach. Moreover, the studio usually has a broad platform, built close to the foot of the frame, about as high as the bottom of the paint frame may be lifted, and wide enough for the step-ladders to rest upon it. The ends of this platform are frequently fitted with vises that it may be used on special occasions as a carpenter's work-bench.

There is one sort of drop that really requires handling on the floor, and that is the sort that shows cut-out foliage, for instance. The foliage to be shown is painted on a canvas drop in the usual manner, and, after being cut away, is mounted, principally with glue, to a curtain made of a coarse netting called scrim, which holds the whole thing in position. Then there are gauzes, finer nettings used to simulate mists and to soften glare of hard lights. They are used also to appear as opaque curtains when lighted from the front, but to melt away in effect, when lighted from the rear, showing the scene behind through them. When just parts of regular canvas are to be made transparent, the old method was to cut out the areas and glue bits of gauze over them; but now there are patent liquid preparations that make a drop transparent wherever they are applied.

As to scene pieces, other than drops and large framed flats, these are painted in any part of the paint room, or paint dock or paint floor, that happens to be convenient. Many of them, like doors, windows and mantels, call for no artistic brushwork, but are painted with no more thought than would be required in touching-up similar affairs in an actual house. One begins to get into "secrets," however, when the painter starts surfacing for imitation stucco work. Preparing a mixture of plaster, glue size and the required color, he dips his brush into it, and then, standing a short distance away from the flat, flight of steps, stone fountain, or whatever the piece may be, he flicks his brush at it so that the stuff spatters in heavy blobs over the area. Tree-trunks and ground surfaces are treated in the same fashion and with the same mixture, save that instead of plaster the painter now uses ordinary sawdust. The canvas or burlap that the builder used to surface the trees and ground, now being soaked with the glue, becomes stiff and fixed in place.

Papier-mâché work is properly done in the paint room, where the molds are usually kept; and here, also, occurs the large-scale plaster-work. Plaster is not greatly favored in stage building because of its weight and its brittleness. It is used far more in the motion picture studios where vastly different conditions admit it. In a film *atelier* the great sphinx that forms so interesting a set piece in one act of Shaw's "Cæsar and Cleopatra," would be reproduced in plaster; for most stages it probably would be devised mainly of canvas and another sort of *papier-mâché* than that previously described in these pages. The original *papier-mâché* seems to have been a French invention of the early eighteenth century. It reached England about the middle of the century, and about twenty years later a native of Birmingham produced an interesting variation which, instead of reducing the paper to pulp, overlaid it in thin sheets glued together. This is the kind now referred to.

The aforementioned sphinx, being perhaps ten feet high and proportionately long—unless its position facing the audience permitted foreshortening—would first have to be conceived in separate parts for portability and storage. Each of these parts would be given its supporting frame, or armature; and over this would be contrived the outward shape. With the usual meshed wire and canvas atop that, much could be done for the broader parts of the body. The face probably would require a clay model with a corresponding plaster "piece-mold"—that is, a mold contrived in several parts for easier handling. This mold, shellacked, and oiled, would then have pressed into it a series of sheets of paper—perhaps even newspaper—that had been soaked in size, one directly over another. About ten sheets would make a tough, strong piece. A brush probably would be used to see that the paper fitted well into the mold, and, perhaps, for some of the more delicate places, like around the eyelids, the first overlay would be not paper but a piece of linen capable of being pressed in without tearing. Plaster-work, on the other hand, would simply attach itself to a cloth base over the armature. It would be very perishable, and its surface would not take paint as easily or as durably as the *papier-mâché*.

Where there is likely to be considerable absorption in the surface as provided by the scene-builder, it should be sized, just as a paperhanger does with a plaster wall before beginning his proper duties. This is commonly done with ordinary glue size with a little whiting mixed in. Sizing has the additional advantage, especially in the case of flats, of tightening the canvas on the frames. Opinions vary about the precise proportions of water and glue in preparing size; but a general agreement specifies that when it is cold it should set like a jelly. Glue for sizing, as procurable at any paint shop, comes in yellow crystals and sells by the pound. It dissolves when boiled in water, and, as remarked, jells when cold. However, it may be added that it has to be stone cold before it becomes thus unusable. The jelly may be made serviceable again merely by heating. The stuff has an evil but not impossible smell, and deteriorates rapidly, especially in warm weather. Spoiling may be checked by the addition of a little carbolic acid. Experiment alone will best determine these points.

Size, as originally prepared, is usually much too strong for regular use, and if applied as is, will shine like varnish and cause objectionable reflections from the lights on the scene. The "working size" is commonly made by taking some of the first-made and adding an equal part of hot water. Too much thinning is dangerous, however, for then the colors with which it is to be mixed will smudge, chip, and rub off. The application of whiting, in with the preliminary coating of size, is of great advantage in providing a clean, uniform surface for the transfer of the design to be painted. But before going into an explanation of that phase of the work, something must be told about the making of the design itself.

For simplest description of the methods involved, it may be assumed that the scene piece to be painted is a simple drop fastened to the paint frame and already sized. The master scenic artist has in hand an approved drawing, in full color, of the piece as it should look when completed, and made to scale, the usual scale in theatre work being a half-inch to the foot. The first step is to pencil off this drawing into inch squares, numbered across the top and down one side for ready identification of parts. The next step is to divide the drop into two-foot squares similarly identified. An artist then mounts the scaffold before the drop, and with the approved drawing in hand, sketches into each big square with a bit of charcoal, what is contained in the corresponding small square. He does not merely outline the forms, but also the masses of light and shade.

This is the least involved way. In many studios the enlargement from the small drawing is either by hand or by means of a pantograph, square by square, upon sheets of manila paper. The lines are then perforated, at intervals of half an inch or so, with small awls or common pins fixed in handles—or yet more speedily with the unthreaded needles of sewing machines or with various patent devices contrived for the purpose. Each sheet of paper thereupon becomes a full-size pattern which is held in place against the canvas while a small "pounce-bag"—a bit of coarse muslin with a handful of powdered charcoal tied in it—is rubbed over the perforations. The pattern being removed, the design is found transferred to the canvas in dotted lines. Ingenious, practical, and traditional. But there is one other more up-to-date way that has much to recommend it. By this method the original drawing is photo-

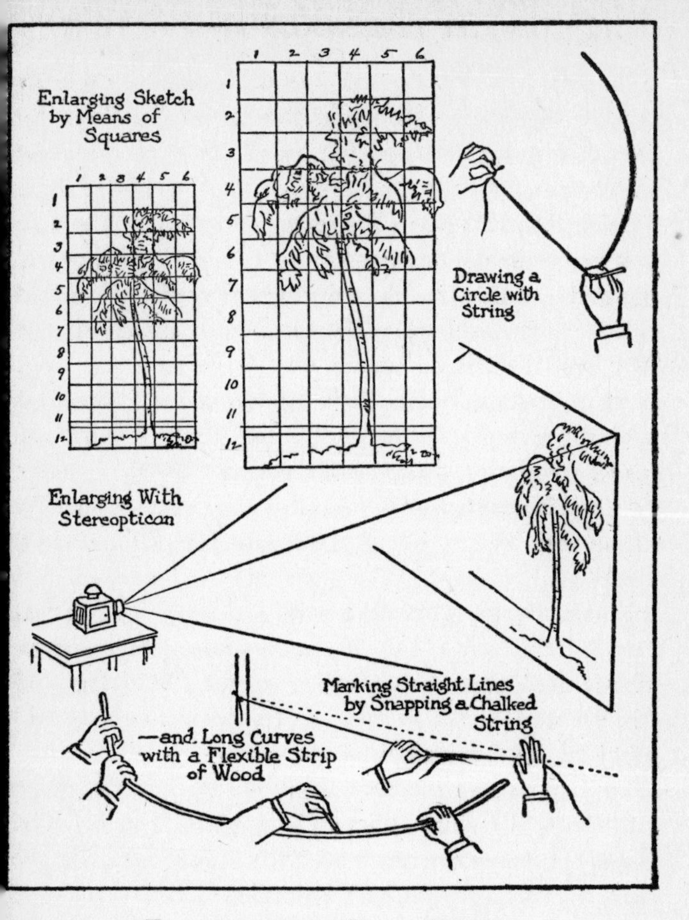

ENLARGING THE SCENE DESIGN

Here again occur wide differences in professional practice. Of all methods named in the body of the text, probably the commonest is enlarging by means of squares, a way frequently to be seen in the work of those artists who paint the large outdoor advertising signs. Nevertheless, the other methods have their champions—and their merits.

graphed upon a lantern slide—in black and white or autochrome, as desired—and then projected upon the canvas with the stereopticon, the artist standing on the scaffold and tracing the design.

When the surface of the scene has only a few simple features to be painted upon it, of course the artist does not go to all this trouble. Straight lines are sometimes ruled, particularly when they are short ones; but for long ones the time-honored way is the snapped cord. A string, rubbed with chalk or charcoal, is stretched against the canvas in the position where the line is to be made. Pulling it out from the canvas the painter releases it suddenly. It strikes the canvas smartly throughout its length, and the impact leaves the desired mark on the canvas. For horizontal lines the sides of the paint frame provide a straight-edge; for vertical lines an ordinary plumb-line serves admirably. Large circles are made with a string across the radius and turned; and curves are sometimes drawn with the aid of a long flexible strip of wood.

For wallpapers methods vary. If the scene is for a stock theatre and is neither to be used for a long period nor to be taken on the road, actual wallpaper may be spread over the flats, the best flats for this purpose being those covered with wall-board. A regular paper-hanger is required by union rules to do this work. If durability is important, the scene-painter stencils the design on the canvas; and this, to judge from the apparent ease with which he manipulates the stencils, is an offhand matter. If the reader thinks it really is so, just let him try it. Anyway, the scene-painter finds the stencil so real a labor-saving device that he often cuts his own. He sometimes also uses the *papier-mâché* ornaments carried in stock by the larger wallpaper houses, and that may be tacked so easily to a flat.

Scenic artists ordinarily describe their colors as "cold-water paints"; but, in politer phrase, they are tempera or distemper colors. The ordinary local paint shop carries them, but usually in pastel shades because there is little call for violent hues. These are procurable, however. Kalsomine pigments of this sort come in powdered form and in bulk, to be retailed at a few cents per pound, some naturally more expensive than others. They are readily soluble in water, the proportions being usually a pint to a pound with the addition of an equal amount of working size to fix it to the surface where it is to be applied. Cold-water paints are as pleasant to use as common water colors, blending readily and capable of effects of great delicacy, as one may see by examining the tempera paintings by the masters.

Brushes are generally of three kinds, broad flat ones for sizing and painting in large areas; stout round ones for brushing in such parts as foliage; and small "liners." A wider variety depends upon individual taste.

Among scenic artists there are just as many "techniques" as among painters anywhere else; and therefore it is impossible to name any single prevailing method. Some believe in blending colors before application. Others contend that a better effect is derived by the "pointilliste" system whereby tiny brush strokes of different raw colors are placed side by side to be blended by the eye of the spectator from a distance. Some maintain a bewildering array of pots that seem to cover the whole range of the spectrum. Others contend that it is easier to light a scene in which all colors in it are derived from three primaries, red, yellow, and blue. These last-named men work with fairly simple equipment, making their greens from yellow and blue, their oranges from red and yellow, their purples from red and blue. The only other paints they have are white and black. Apparently there is no powdered black easily soluble in water; so black is the one paint that usually comes in especially prepared, liquid form, this, however, readily to be thinned with water.

The ordinary painter, who does the actual painting in on the canvas, naturally cannot be permitted to adopt a marked technique of his own. The whole scene must be uniform in its effect, while in all probability many painters will work separately upon its parts. Technique is established by the original, master artist; the lesser workers are at pains to imitate that. In these circumstances a very familiar difficulty is to keep the setting, which may consist of fifteen to fifty pieces, in a single key.

Probably the greatest difficulty is to prejudge colors as they will appear under the stage lights. That this is important will be appreciated by any one who has asked a shopkeeper to bring a necktie or a bit of ribbon out to the doorway where it might be seen by daylight. On the old stages the great consideration was quantity of light; there is now superadded to this, the vital question of quality. Lamps that seem to give plenty of light may shed rays predominating in blues, yellows or reds with consequently different effects on the scenery. Many fine distinctions may be drawn in this regard;

but where an attraction has to travel from one theatre to another, and the scene must stand up under varying conditions, some compromise is only reasonable. In usual circumstances, then, the scene-painter may intensify his blues and yellows, for these tend to be obscured, and to soften his reds and greens, for these frequently become more vigorous under the lights.

To understand the tendencies of modern scene-painting, one must refer to the outstanding differences in color work in the greater field of art. Painters of today have learned to paint with light—that is, to know that shadows are not dull and soggy but are filled with reflected illuminations. Hence, preferred practice seems to be to paint shadows in colors complementary to those of the light. Thus, if the pervading light of the setting is yellow, the shadows would be blue; if green, the shadows would be purple—and so on. In scene-painting, especially, artists have learned another lesson, which is that heavily painted shadows require a serious excess of lighting to show them up, meaning a fierce glare that produces other shadows of an unwanted kind. By painting the shadows with lighter colors and illuminating them with meager lights, the desired effect may be obtained without detriment to the rest of the scene.

Fireproofing the scene-pieces is commonly done after they are fully painted. Fireproofing mixtures are usually sprayed upon the pieces from the back so as not to affect the surface colors, although most of the patent preparations claim not to damage the scenery in any way in any circumstances.

Out of the painter's province frequently come miscellaneous properties that have to be especially built—like peculiar chairs and tables or a *papier-mâché* roasted turkey—either because of expense or because real ones would be too heavy; but of course whenever such pieces are procurable at reasonable prices and in desirable condition in real life, they are purchased or rented. Those that are especially made, or that are bought outright, are kept in the property-room after the production that brought them to the theatre has run its course, pending other calls for them. Hence the property-room is a veritable old curiosity shop, and frequently contains valuable articles originally picked up for a song.

In these days of expensive real estate, it costs real money to maintain things in storage. The articles must be kept dry and protected from theft, fire, moths, and other vermin; and there are more costly considerations to be added to the possibility that the articles may never be needed again. Rental is therefore becoming more and more the expedient course. The furniture dealer is frequently willing to lend a limited number of his wares for acknowledgment in the program. If the demand is large, the established rental is ten per cent of the value per week. If the rental mounts up, in the course of a long run, to the actual market value or perhaps five per cent more, which would be fair in installment buying, the dealer sometimes yields title to the manager. Or he may be willing to buy back after a time, at a discount, goods that he sold outright at the start.

Establishments in the larger producing centers frequently make a business of supplying props in this way, their stocks, of course, embracing many odd things that no ordinary dealer could reasonably be expected to carry. Properties for period settings are almost always to be had, to some extent, from the professional costumers.

CHAPTER VIII

LIGHTS

STAGE lighting equipment becomes easier to think about when considered in five general divisions—those lamps that light the stage from the auditorium; the footlights in front of the curtain-line; the border-lights overhead and the portable lights that may occur almost anywhere.

Auditorium lights for stage effect are usually situated behind and above the last and highest row of seats in the balcony or gallery. They are almost invariably spotlights the rays of which may be focused upon a single performer or spread to include the entire scene. In theatres where vaudeville or musical comedy prevails, the equipment in this position is considerable, three or four powerful lamps of the same description being ranged there side by side. Used to follow a singer or dancer about the stage a spotlight obviously is just a useful convention, frankly helping the audience to concentrate its attention upon one subject. On the other hand, in any effort to create scenic illusion, the balcony light is valuable mainly as a "flood."

Successfully to throw a light for a distance of perhaps more than a hundred feet, from source to object, means a relatively strong lamp. Its carrying power depends upon the spread of its rays. When they are drawn together to illuminate a small area, that area will

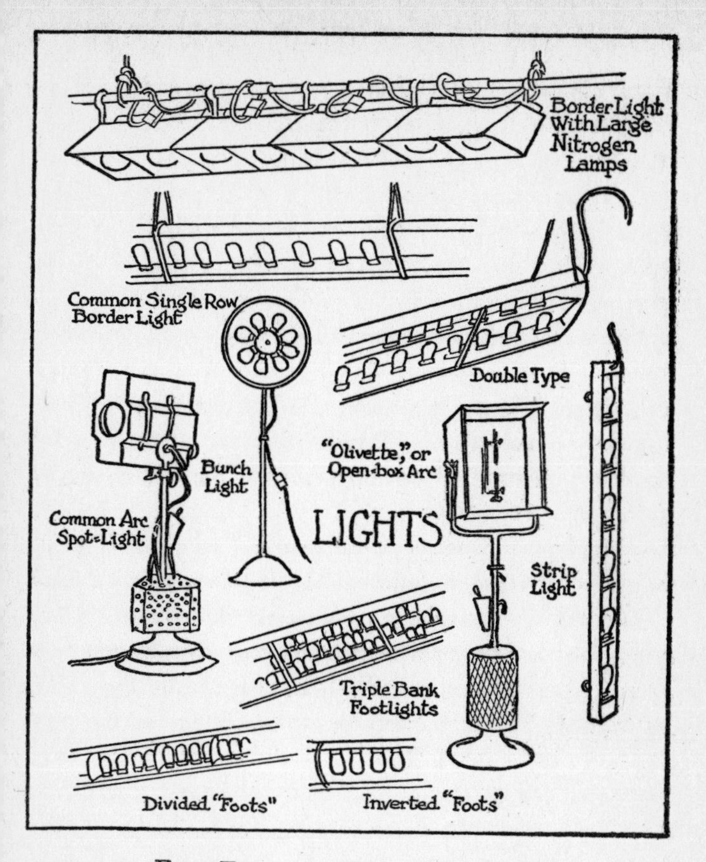

FIVE FORMS OF STAGE LIGHTING

The trained electrician ranks as high for engineering knowledge as any other person in the working theatre organization. He does not always fulfill requirements, but when he does his expertness is wholly admirable. Without his coöperation the finest work of the modern scene-painter goes for naught, and the actor is compelled to struggle against overwhelming odds. In his own department he is known sometimes as Tom, Dick or Harry, but more often as "Juice."

naturally be brighter than when the rays are spread to include everything else on the scene. Hence, in many theatres where the balcony lamps are used just for flooding, they are moved down to the front of the balcony itself so that the "throw" is cut approximately in half, giving the stage the benefit of more light for less power. A flood light of this sort usually has a fixed focus and may be operated from the stage switchboard.

It may be so controlled only when it is an incandescent lamp. That is to say, the law generally permits remote control of only that kind because of the fire risk of a naked arc. The approved arc light calls for a fairly elaborate construction and a separate attendant. In principle it consists of two carbon pencils, set at an angle point to point and in line with each other, each connected with one end of an electric circuit. When the points are touched to complete the circuit, and then drawn apart, the current leaps the gap in the form of a dazzling light which continues until one or the other of the carbons is burned away. As the distance between the pencils must be evenly maintained, for steadiness of light, and at the same time the faster-burning positive pencil must be fed into the arc, constant adjustment is necessary. In earlier years the attendant took care of that; but now there are ingenious mechanisms that make the lamp automatic. Nevertheless the attendant must be there, because even small variations in current will reduce the arc, till the carbon points touch, following which the light will go out and have to be started over again.

The spread of the rays from the arc is governed by moving the arc itself toward and away from the condensing lens that fronts the lamp. Opening the spread, of course, weakens the illumination at the same time; but this is valuable for variation in effects. To cut off the spread where it is not needed for a weak light, the arc sometimes is equipped in front of the condenser with an iris diaphragm such as is used, on a much smaller scale, to cut down the light aperture in a camera. So, when a spotlight has to be weakened in intensity, without altering the area of illumination, the arc must be moved simultaneously closer to its condensing lens as the iris closes in.

The nitrogen or gas-filled incandescent lamp, of from 500 to 1500 watts, is much less complicated. It is controlled in virtually the same way as an ordinary fifty or sixty watt bulb in one's own home. To dim it a rheostat is merely introduced into the circuit, in this case, at the switchboard. With a couple of such lamps, fixed in reflectors to the front of the balcony rail, the average small stage can have flood lighting quite as good as any.

Footlights present more complicated problems. One of the first of these is the moot point of whether or not there should be any footlights at all, the answer to which is that sometimes there should be and sometimes there shouldn't. The mere fact that there are occasions when they are vitally needed is sufficient excuse for including them in the permanent installation, and, for chronic objectors to their being, there is a kind that may be turned under the level of the stage floor when not wanted. The need, when it comes, is based upon that same fact, mentioned in the preceding chapter as so profoundly influencing modern art, that in shadows there is a vast amount of reflected light. In the great outdoors the powerful light of the sun is diffused over an almost inconceivable distance; the master of stage lighting could not obtain the same effect from an overhead lamp without making it an offensive and unreal glare. But with a softer overhead light and a lifting of the shadows by means of a floor light, he can create a truer illusion of nature than with no footlights at all. The old hypothetical question, of how one would go about lighting the face of a beautiful woman wearing a big "picture" hat, without the use of footlights, still suggests its own pointed answer.

Footlights are, of course, controlled from the switchboard, not an easy thing to do when the curtain is down and conceals them from the electrician—unless there is some such provision, for his peeping out at them, as was described in the opening chapter on stage arrangement. They are ordinarily in three to four sections, from side to side, depending on the width of the stage, each section separately operated or not as desired. Distinct circuits also regulate white, red, yellow (amber) and blue lamps, with switches and dimmers. White light, added to any color or combination of colors, gives tints; and, of course, shades are provided by dimming. Special colors may be obtained with bulb stains; but stains fade whereas colored glass does not. If the play action is well forward on the scene, the "foots" are sometimes screened with silk to prevent glare.

In bygone years so much depended upon footlights that it is only natural that, when other forms of illumination became more perfected, their emphasis was felt to be undue. They needed toning-down. Therefore, in the better metropolitan "intimate" theatres, the footlights are to be found occupying less than two-thirds of their former space. Their glow is directed mainly to the lower middle part of the scene, which obviously cannot be fully reached otherwise without forcing by the side and top lights. This little trick, of picking up and strengthening a gentle light so that it has the effect of penetrating further, is certainly valid enough, and may find its justification in the higher canons of art.

The diffused light of nature is the excellent example, soft and yet all-pervading. When a producer like Belasco, or his master electrician of these many years, Louis Hartman, provides relays on the scene, disguised in various unobtrusive ways, for carrying the streams of light on and on, there is a discerning mind at work, and it calls for admiration. The Belasco examples are especially notable because they represent the triumph not of a single department of stage work, but a blending of all. His lighting devices are not merely of the scene but serve double and often triple duty in demands of the play action. The screen that softens the glare of the flood-light outside the window happens also to be a sash-curtain; the reflector, that sends a soft radiance into the dark alcove, may be a lovely scarf, thrown carelessly across the piano, to be carried away by one of the characters when that radiance is no longer needed.

It was in the search for the beauties of diffused lighting that the horizont was devised. It takes a light, that is hard and glaring only because it must be bright and at the same time held unreasonably close to the thing it is intended to illuminate, and breaks it up into luminous mist. The loveliest light, the modern artist will say, and say truly, is reflected light. At the close of the nineteenth century the artist Mariano Fortuny carried the idea into color, and instead of screening the stage lights with colored mediums (although he did this too, upon occasion), threw their illumination against colored banners and thence to a plaster dome. To blend one with another, he merely serried the edges of the banners and overlapped them more and more so that the colored reflections merged gradually.

Nevertheless, given due distance, a light will diffuse itself. Certain lights on the stage actually have this advantage. Which suggests the point that there is no single kind of lighting that will serve *all* the purposes of a play. Everything depends on the requirements. Sometimes footlights are needed; sometimes they are not; sometimes spotlights are highly useful, and again they are to be avoided as the plague. One must be reasonable on the subject.

The usual top lights are border-lights, or light-battens. One of these, in its simplest form, is just a sort of inverted metal gutter, or trough, which acts as a reflector for a long row of incandescent bulbs set into it. Three to eight of these borders ordinarily succeed each other at five or six foot intervals above the stage from the proscenium arch to the back wall, running from side to side. They are suspended from pipe battens hung from the gridiron. Electric current reaches them through flexible cables at one side—usually that most convenient to the switchboard—with enough "play" to permit them to be raised and lowered. They are, of course, on counterweighted lines like the drops.

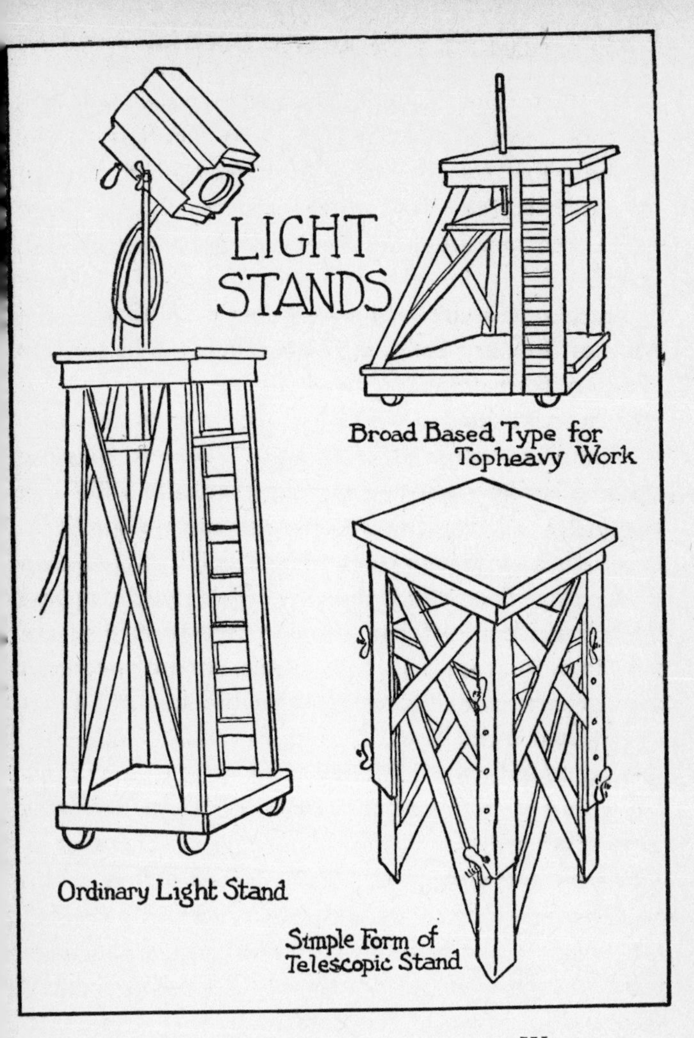

PORTABLE STANDS FOR BACKSTAGE WORK

In a more complex type the border has two rows of lamps on four distinct circuits, one white lights, the second amber, the third red and the fourth blue. Moreover each border is usually divided into three or four lateral sections for separate control from the switchboard.

Some stages employ border-lights consisting not of rows of ordinary bulbs, but of a single line of perhaps a dozen powerful nitrogen lamps, each in a separate compartment fronted with a colored medium, and each individually controlled. In other theatres may be found a border consisting of a pipe batten to which are clamped a number of ordinary automobile spotlights turned as necessary to concentrate areas of illumination on the stage floor. In many of the little theatres appear borders made up of lamps and reflectors such as are used in store windows. Still another kind of overhead arrangement is the "dome," not the horizont but a sort of inverted metal bowl, four or five feet in diameter, serving as reflector for one strong light or a number set within it. If the bulbs are small ones, there may be as many as twenty-five or thirty, giving a beautifully diffused light, usually over the middle of the stage, but also over any other part desired.

In naming the five general divisions of stage lighting equipment, the lights at the sides of the proscenium arch were included among the portables. They generally are of that character; and yet in many of the newer theatres the side lights are built in as permanent fixtures. In form they are identical with what are commonly called strip-lights. Their construction, as a rule, is that of a long flat narrow box, such as an umbrella comes in, made of metal, of course, and with recesses, one above another, each designed to hold one ordinary incandescent bulb. The recesses are painted white the better to reflect the light. Length of the strip-light is indeterminate, although seldom longer than ten feet or shorter than three. Some forms provide bulb recesses one to the foot, while others accommodate three or four in that same space. Rings or hooks on the back are frequently provided that the strip may be "tied off" in any given position. The strip is exceedingly serviceable for many purposes. It may be placed over the outside of a door to light a backing, or on the floor back of a profile strip to kill shadows, or in many other places that readily suggest themselves as the needs arise.

The spotlight has already been described. Backstage it is regarded as a portable, and may be found in many different positions as occasion demands. Sometimes it is mounted in the fly-gallery to penetrate to the stage through the wings; again it may be placed on a light-stand to shoot its rays across the top of the wall of a room; at other times it may rest on the stage floor to pick out something high up on the scene. There also are what are called "baby" spots, or "chasers," these being little lenses backed by 500 watt nitrogen lamps, small enough to be tucked away in the footlight trough or perched on the rail of the fly-gallery, and used frequently to light individual players in certain "key" positions on the stage.

Chief among the other portable lights are the "olivettes" or open-box floods. They are square-headed lamps, on stands, the light unit being either a powerful nitrogen bulb or one or two arcs, and having no lens intervening between it and the object to be illuminated. Indeed they are not expected to illuminate any single object, but just to flood a given area with bright light. The only other portable offstage lamps, that need be mentioned in this running account, are the bunch-lights, consisting of square or round reflector-heads mounted on standards, each head accommodating half a dozen or more ordinary incandescent bulbs. Their use is to flood also, but with milder light.

Now arises the question of how these portables are connected with the electric current. At various places in the stage floor, or in metal boxes along the wall, are pockets into which the small cables, with which all of these lamps are provided, may be plugged. Of course the pockets are controlled from the switchboard. Another convenience is what is called a plugging-box, attached to a heavy cable that in turn is connected with a convenient outlet from the main. It may be placed almost anywhere on the scene, and its two to twelve sockets (rarely more than four) will accommodate a corresponding number of lamp leads.

Lamps used as part of the scene, on tables or on the floor beside the piano or easy chair, are joined outside the scene in the same manner. Wall-bracket lights are usually wired with just a short cable terminating, on the off-stage side of the flat, with one end of a "connector," the other end being attached to a lead reaching to the plugging-box. As to the chandelier, the top of which is drawn up through a hole in the ceiling-piece, that fixture is served by a plug connector, of the same general type, that hangs at idle times at the end of a cable in the flies.

There are always variations and new ideas; but the touring companies pick them up as they travel from place to place and spread the news. Consequently, what has been sketched here, as a good average working equipment of lights, may be accepted as really representative. Lighting engineers will have their better recommendations that in time will be realized in practice. Until then, however, an equipment of this sort may be adopted as a practical start based on the experience of men actually engaged, in this day and age, in meeting and solving these problems.

CHAPTER IX

MECHANICAL EFFECTS

In mechanical departments backstage the word "effect" has a very especial meaning. And yet it is so general in its application there that it is difficult to define. In a very broad sense it may be said to consist of any impression produced upon an audience by mechanical means. There are lighting effects and wind and rain effects and train and automobile effects and as many more as there are such impressions in real life. From this it is easy to understand why they defy classification.

What complicates the problem is that there is no universal agreement as to the nature of the appliances necessary. Were it not for the fact that regular supply houses provide excellent devices for stage effects ready-made, probably such articles would never be the same in any two theatres. But even despite this certain standardization, the backstage handy-men still invent ingenious contraptions the like of which were never seen before on land or sea.

It must be borne in mind that the stage invention is to be used in very peculiar circumstances. It sometimes is of more genuine effect than an actual demonstration of nature would be under the same conditions. Real water, for instance, may easily destroy its own stage illusion. There has been current in the theatre for years the story of a veteran property-man who saw Niagara Falls for the first time. When asked what he thought of that grand sight he replied contemptuously that he could make a much better effect with a wheel-barrow and a piece of tin. The amazing part of the story is that he probably could—as far as the theatre is concerned.

In the old days of the theatre the property-man and the stage carpenter were the chief magicians in such matters, standing ready to produce the call of the cuckoo or a sunset, "battle alarums and excursions" or a *papier-mâché* banquet; but to-day the work devolves upon the division men in each sharply-defined department. The electrician devises effects, that he and his comrades must operate, just as the property-man provides only those things for which he is responsible "on set." That engineering principles are more elaborate to-day, and that specialists necessarily know more about the labor-saving instruments in their own lines, probably have much to do with it. That sprite, Electricity, that puts a girdle around the earth in a fraction of the time required by the immortal Puck, operates from a distance, when the stage manager at his prompt-table merely touches buttons there, machines producing wind, thunder, and lightning.

Effects of nature are probably the oldest in the theatre. They may be found, not only in the Orphic mysteries of ancient Greece, but also in the earlier tribal initiation ceremonies of primitive man. In the theatre of Æschylus, Euripides, and Sophocles, prismatic mirrors, flashing in the sun, simulated lightning from Olympus; leaden balls, bounced on stretched leather, rumbled the fabled wrath of Jove.

A sound of rushing, whistling wind, as successfully produced by De Loutherbourg for the theatre of David Garrick at the close of the eighteenth century, was made by rubbing two silk-covered discs together; and this remains perhaps the simplest of the good ways of giving the effect. If one will run his nails with a rotary movement over a tightly stretched cloth of any kind, he will illustrate the principle. For stages where there is plenty of room for cumbrous pieces, the same idea is demonstrated with a large wooden cylinder turned with a crank against a strip of canvas pulled over it. A more up-to-date device, that makes plenty of noise without occupying much space, is a small siren turned by hand to give the desired gradations.

The appearance of wind is given by electric fans; but care must be taken that the fans are noiseless in operation. In motion picture studios where there is no accompanying sound record, producers may use whole batteries of airplane propellers. Not so on the stage; and consequently there is greater dependence in that realm on the director's ingenuity. For an appearance of wind there must be something for the wind to blow. On this account the effect depends upon throwing articles into the air-current—dead leaves, papers, waving branches, curtains and so on as these may be relevant to the scene.

Thunder effects have evolved through centuries of experiment. In addition to the primitive tympanum or "tempestuous drum," there is the celebrated "roll'd bullet" of Shakespearean days. To some minds this

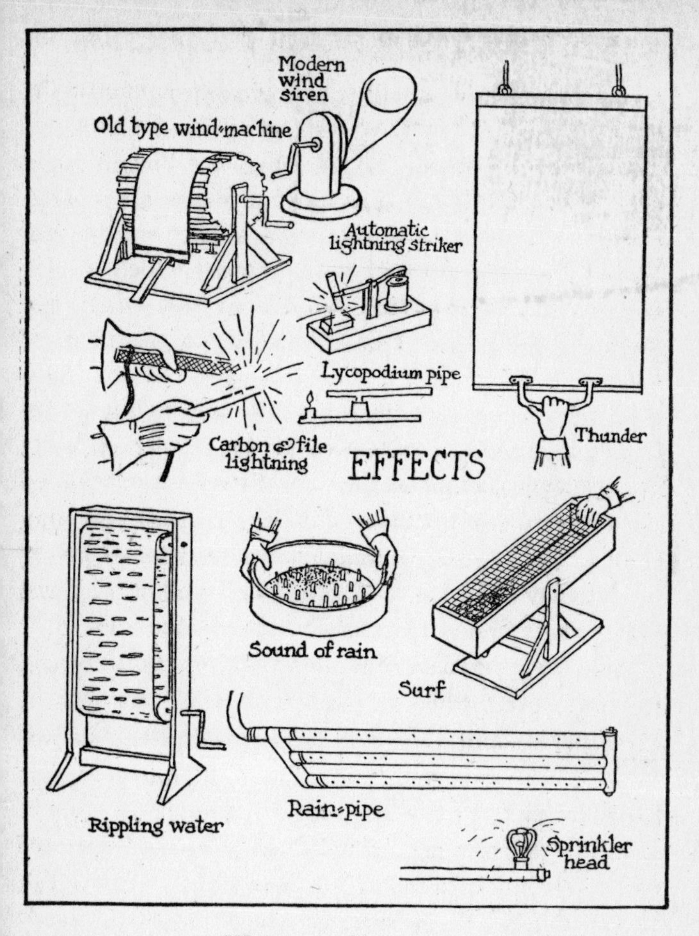

WEATHER EFFECTS

Most of these simple devices have interesting histories. The thunder sheet is chief monument to the memory John Dennis, the critic who invented it, while the old wind-machine, surf-box and rippling water effect recall David Garrick's scene-painter, De Loutherbourg.

meant rolling cannon balls along the upper floor of the stage—and no doubt that very thing was impressively done; but it seems also to have meant rolling them in a barrel rotated in a frame by means of a crank, considerably more practicable from many standpoints. Next came the "mustard-bowl" variety which, as far as one may judge, was a concave wooden affair containing iron balls and either rocked on the floor or rotated by hand in a horizontal plane. It may also have been suspended by ropes like a hanging flower basket, a rather obvious thing to do. However, these devices, as ingenious as they are, have been supplanted generally by the famous thunder invented by John Dennis, the English theatrical critic. He devised it for his tragedy "Appius and Virginia," damned by the public at its first performance at Drury Lane in 1708. Dennis always looked upon this thunder as his especial property, even when he had no further use for it. He bitterly—and of course properly—resented its unlicensed use. His complaint "That's my thunder!" has taken its place in the language as a figure of speech. But, for effectiveness coupled with convenience, his useful invention probably has never been superseded. It was simply a large sheet of copper suspended vertically and shaken from the edge.

The thunder-clap has been regarded as a separate feature. Its traditional stage form consists of a half-dozen or so iron plates hung one above another at intervals of a foot or two on cords. Each plate is perforated in the same way, with a couple of holes, and through these descend lines from pulleys above, made fast to the bottom plate. Pulling the lines sharply brings the plates together with a crash.

Lightning is another interesting development. Fired resin was one of the early forms. But what seems to have been the first real instrument for the purpose was the lycopodium pipe. Lycopodium, as procurable at the neighborhood pharmacy, is a powder made of the spores of a common plant, used medicinally as a dusting-powder for injured skin, but having the property, when ignited, of going off with a flash. The lycopodium pipe is made principally of a long tube, the middle of which opens into a small box of the powder, while a candle burns at a set distance from the far end. The operator, blowing into the near end, creates a suction which draws some of the powder into the pipe and sends it flying across against the flame. This principle is still used, at times, to represent bursts of flame from a blacksmith's forge. The "magnesium gun" employs the same idea. One of the performances of Meyerbeer's opera "L'Africaine," years ago, was said to have had no lightning simply because a boy, delegated to blow the lycopodium pipe, took a starting breath so deep that he inhaled the powder—"swallowed the lightning," as they said.

With the coming of electricity lightning was made with its own element. Action of an arc light, described in the preceding chapter, must have suggested the old carbon-and-file variety which still provides the effect now and then. It is said to have been originated by that prolific inventor of stage effects, Lincoln J. Carter. Here a pencil of carbon and a common iron file are connected with the respective ends of an ordinary lamp circuit. The operator, wearing stout rubber gloves as an obvious precaution, rubs carbon and file together. Irregularities of the file make a variable contact, and a fine spluttering and flare result. In modern equipment the "lightning-striker" is a tiny see-saw, at one end of which is a carbon that rests against a metal block, and at the other a small electro-magnet that pulls it down and consequently starts the arc and holds it as long as the circuit is complete. Strikers of this sort are usually placed in different parts of the flies and operated with push-buttons from the prompter's desk.

Stage rain usually is real water. A filled tank is placed somewhere in the flies high enough to lend force of gravity; and the water descends therefrom through a hose to a single, double or triple rainpipe—a horizontal pipe, up among the borders, with a line of small perforations at intervals of about an inch. If the rain is supposed to cover the scene, this pipe extends the full width of the stage close to the curtain-line. The water is caught below, in an improvised gutter edged with tarpaulins, descending therefrom, through an opening in the stage, to probably an ordinary vinegar barrel in the cellar. Rain that is just to be seen through a window is much simpler. In this case the tank may rest on a platform to feed a pipe fastened just above the window, and the water may be caught in a wash-boiler, or something equally convenient, at the floor level. Great care must be exercised to keep water from spilling into the electric floor-pockets of the stage. In fact, this danger is one that impels builders frequently to put the pockets against the wall a couple of feet above the floor.

The sound of raindrops may be made with some dried peas or buckshot in a common, round, uncovered cheese-box. Dropping the peas or shot into the box, a few at a time, starts the rain; and then, moving the box with a rotary action so that the contents roll around and around, gives the steady downpour. A refinement of this device is to set a number of thin wooden sticks upright in the box that the whirling missiles may strike them with sharp *tics,* continuing the suggestion of individual raindrops. Another improvement is to mount the box on a gear that it may be turned with a crank at the side.

Rainbows may be counterfeited by decomposing a beam of white light with a prism after the famous example set by Sir Isaac Newton. Mists are most successfully represented by gauze curtains; and, if they are moving mists intended to lift out of sight, the curtains should have no battens at the bottom, while the bottoms should be cut in jagged lines. Sprites of the air are made to fly by means of counterweighted piano wires fastened to harnesses on the fairies' backs.

Moving clouds are virtually all stereopticon effects, and, quite generally, are automatic in operation. Attached to the stereopticon is a shallow circular box in which may be placed a large gelatine disc with its edge just covering the lens. Upon this edge are painted the clouds, or they may be reproduced from photographic plates. A clock-work mechanism revolves the disc; and, as it turns, the stereopticon projects the traveling image. Many interesting effects are produced by using combinations of two or more stereopticons, outfitted in this manner. The projection principle provides waterfalls, effects of swimming fish or under-water scenes, sunsets, moon and star details, fire and smoke, rain, rainbows, snow, and much more. To show these the stage requires darkening, but only in part and that part merely dimmed.

To obtain other effects there are especial attachments for the olivette and for the spotlight. For the former there are colored gelatine screens and bands of silk mounted on rollers, to be turned as day shades into night or night lightens to dawn. For the spot there is principally the color-wheel, mounted so that its edge may be turned at any speed to screen the light with its varicolored segments.

However, one must remember that successful projection means that nothing may interfere between projector and image. The stereopticon may set at the rear of the scene and the image thrown against a transparent curtain; but if that image is to be seen by the audience, there must be no strong light in front. In that event the actors must walk about in semi-darkness, seen mostly in silhouette. These considerations present the case against those magic lantern enthusiasts who foresee a time when all stage scenery will be made in this fashion.

The sun is rarely if ever presented directly upon the scene; but the moon is shown often. Projection serves very well for this because a night scene is naturally darkened. At the same time there is a simpler way with some especial advantages. It is represented in the justly-celebrated "moon box." This is a cornucopia, the large end of which is of approximately the desired size of the moon, and the small

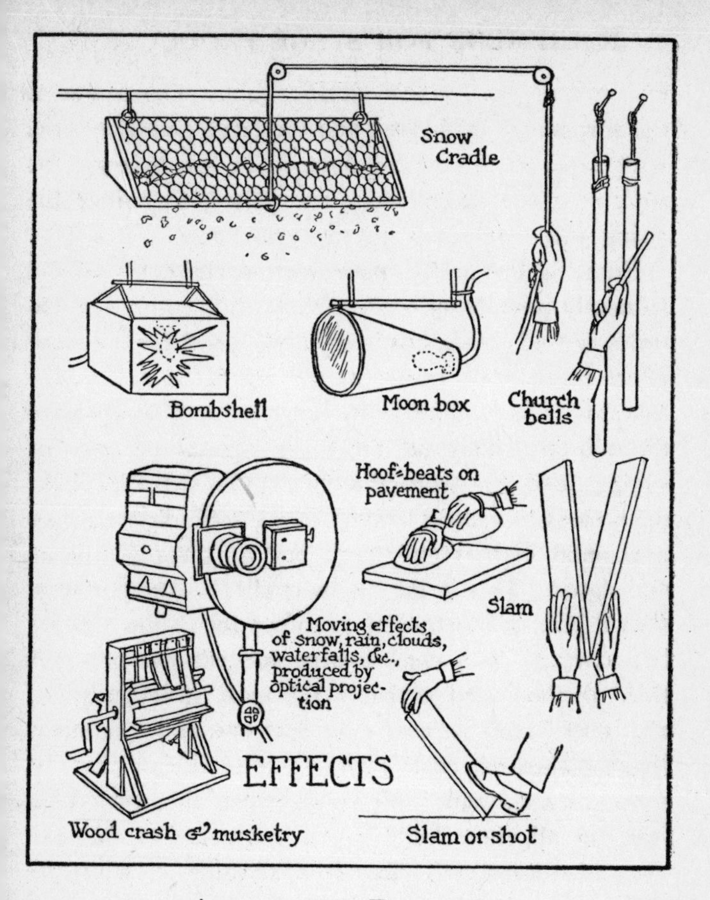

Alarums and Excursions

Effects principally of sound but with four for sight. The "bombshell" is of the latter sort. Sound of the explosion is to be made separately elsewhere while in the box, hanging in mid-air over the night scene, the electric light is flashed on and off. This effect seems to have been one of the recent inventions developed for plays of the World War.

end containing a single electric bulb. The inside of the cornucopia is silvered and the large end is covered with paper to diffuse the light. The effect is worked back of a transparent drop and raised, to imitate the rising orb, with lines to the gridiron.

Snow is ordinarily made with paper cut fine and so nearly resembling confetti that white confetti sometimes is used. Asbestos is especially good for the snow effect provided it is not to fall upon the actors, for asbestos is very difficult to brush off. But whatever the substance may be, there are various devices for sifting it down from the flies. One of the oldest methods is to make a loop of coarse scrim between two horizontal battens and work one of them gently up and down. This is the "snow-cradle." Another way, shown here in illustration, is to put the "snow" into a box covered with chicken-wire and tilt the box. A third method, and probably the most satisfactory of all, is to have two coarse screens one above another, shaking them alternately from side to side so that the snow sifts through. However, when the snow does start to fall, the effect is much heightened if fans are directed toward each other from the sides to whirl the flakes.

Where loose snow must be picked up from the ground, or kicked about the scene, the material is usually coarse white salt. For snow on clothing the salt is dampened. For snow on branches and around window-panes, cotton is the rule. For frosting on the panes they are painted with a saturated solution of medicinal salts which crystallize beautifully.

Coarse salt also simulates ocean spray, being thrown

into the air by a stagehand situated behind some convenient masking piece. The actual surf is rarely shown, although, when it has to be, there is an interesting device in the form of a long narrow roller, running from side to side of the scene, with four wide, longitudinal flaps, each painted to represent a wave. When this roller is turned continuously toward the audience, there is a certain sense of the waves coming in. In all events, the device ere now has produced thunders of applause. Fairly calm water is indicated with colored oilcloth and light effects projected upon it, and still more ingeniously with a strip of lightly-stretched green silk blown from the side by an electric fan. Ocean waves are shown as painted profile strips, moved from side to side by stagehands in the wings, assisted by light effects of various kinds.

The old way to represent the deep was for a number of stagehands to get on their hands and knees under a green floor-cloth and work it up and down. A story relates that, on an occasion of this kind when the scene purported to show a naval battle, one of the stagehands accidentally put his startled head through a rotten spot in the canvas. But before the audience could realize it, a quick-witted actor on one of the ships cried "Man overboard!" and hauled him to the deck.

Appearance of surf is one thing; its sound is another. The most successful noise of surf is made with a long shallow box, balanced on a frame like a see-saw, about a quarter filled with loose shells or broken bits of crockery, the top covered with meshed wire, and tilted up at first one end and then the other. The same general sound may be produced by wrapping a couple of wooden blocks with sandpaper and rubbing them over a board with a rotary motion, or using a pair of stiff scrubbing-brushes in the same way; but it's lots harder work. Sometimes the shells or crockery are revolved in a broad wheel, which is more difficult to time in its operation than the teeter. The wheel effect is at its best when used to imitate the sound of water pouring into a bathtub.

Rippling reflections of lights on water may be projected by stereopticon; but a very excellent way is that, shown in illustration, whereby a continuously moving vertical band, with transverse slits in it, is placed between a strong light and the back of the scene. One side of the band ascending as the other comes down, and the light going through only as the slits on both sides come into line, this illusion is one of the most pleasing and generally satisfactory of the large number in the stage artificer's box of tricks.

Fires—that is, conflagrations—are mostly stereopticon effects in various combinations. Olivettes and spots, with appropriate color mediums fitted to them, contribute much. Colored tongues of silk, blown by electric fans, make excellent flames there (as they do in a stage fireplace); ingenious systems of bolts and latches release falling parts of the doomed house; smokepots provide clouds of smoke if that is needed; mechanical "crickets" or "whizzers," such as happy crowds use on New Year's Eve, turned slowly and irregularly, provide the ominous crackling, and small lights flashed on and off suggest the glow of charred wood. The whole impression of chaos is usually increased by heavy bombs set off at intervals; but nobody seems to know precisely why.

A smokepot is procurable from the manufacturer of fireworks. It is a small pasteboard cylinder, from about half an inch to an inch in diameter and in length from six inches to a foot or so, the size depending upon the time required for its action, which is commonly from half a minute to four minutes. It is lighted in the middle, and, at that point only, the smoke promptly pours forth. It may be held with complete safety in the hand until it goes out.

In battle scenes the bombs are important and may be worked up to crescendo effects. Visible explosions are commonly contrived with springboards tied down and laden with débris, to be tripped suddenly on cue with ordinary closet latches, the noise being made separately. Rattle of musketry, or even the *rat-tat-tat* of a machine-gun, is nothing more serious, as a rule, than a wooden cylinder, built on the "cricket" principle, that engages, and then, as it turns, sharply releases, a number of flexible slats. A bass or "bull" drum is unexcelled for distant cannon. For the single sharp shot offstage, a blank cartridge fired by a revolver is the rule; but a short board held up on end and then slapped down violently with the foot is just as noisy and less trouble. And, as for the dust of battle that the colonel's messenger brushes so realistically from his uniform as he enters after that long hard ride of so many miles, it's only fuller's earth. The sound of horse's hoofs has been made for generations by blocks of wood (and of later years by cocoanut shells) beaten on the floor. This, however, is the sound of hoofs on a pavement.

When the animal is presumed to be moving over bare ground, the beats are made with a rug under the blocks.

A crash of glass is the sharp shake of a container of some sort partly filled with broken glass. To give the sound full vent the container usually is covered only with meshed wire. Breaking wood is its own best imitator; but there deserves to be mentioned the patent "breakaway door" which can apparently be battered to pieces with a sledge-hammer and subsequently be restored for smashing again at the next performance.

The theatre vacuum-cleaner makes the purr of the motor-car and sometimes the overhead drone of the airplane, although the latter is much better simulated by thrusting a tightly folded newspaper against the whirling blades of an electric fan. Ordinary flashlights make the lamps of the automobile as it turns up the driveway toward the house. Its signal—horn, siren or whatever it may be—is imitated by the actual device sounded by a stagehand from out in the alley, to give it distance, and then brought closer to the scene.

Railroad trains, when shown in full, are usually painted on a long canvas unrolled from a vertical drum at one side of the stage and rolled on a second one at the other. When the train comes toward the audience, the stage is usually darkened to conceal the device which consists in the main of the locomotive collapsed against the wall. The headlight, provided with an iris diaphragm which is at first nearly closed, starts down near the floor to suggest the train approaching from the distance. Then it is raised vertically on a string, the iris being gradually opened at the same time until the light is full size and in its proper position, at which juncture the telescoped parts begin opening out.

The bell is just a long metal tube hanging on the back of some nearby flat and struck with a small bar or mallet. Church bells are of the same kind, the notes determined by the length and diameter of the tubes. The sound of the locomotive otherwise is largely the work of a stagehand who provides the steam. He is busily engaged in beating a large piece of stovepipe with two long flexible wire brushes. Noise of the wheels, clanking of the rods and the general rumble, call for the joint efforts of several other men who variously work the thunder curtain, tap a block of metal with light hammers, and drag chains and other metal miscellany, tied together, around the floor.

There are countless small effects listed in the stage worker's experience that are difficult to classify. To boil water on a stove that has no fuel, he uses the preparation known as "canned heat"; or, if all desired is to show steam from the spout of the kettle, he puts into the kettle, in a little water, a bit of "dry ice" (solidified carbon dioxide). To "burn" a stick of wood in a stove, he fits the inside of the stove with flashing electric bulbs, some tongues of red, yellow and blue silk and an electric fan to blow them upward. To burn papers in a fireplace that probably has no real heat to it, a stagehand stands behind to light them with a taper and to see that no real damage is done.

CHAPTER X

THE STAGE CREW

For many years the three natural divisions of the stage crew have been recognized as scenery, property, and lighting. It is only in the present day of organized labor that they have had formal delimitation.

Each division of the modern crew has its leader or "boss." To him all persons of his department are responsible. The smallest division is usually the property section, consisting normally of head property man and one assistant. If the chief's duties are considerable, he may also have three or four "clearers," that is, unskilled workers to carry off furniture, rugs, pictures, and so forth that come in the property man's province—to dismantle the set, in other words.

The general definition of property, in the theatrical sense, is any object that *looks to the audience* to be portable. For instance, a piano, or a screen, or a curtain, or a wine-glass, is known by the spectator to be portable from his own real-life experience. He does not, however, comprehend carrying around the built-in wash-tubs and the kitchen stove, which is, nevertheless, actually done by the stage crew. Some of these distinctions are not yet completely drawn. At about the close of the first decade of the present century a difficult one—about whether a fountain is a set piece or a property—almost caused a permanent rift between

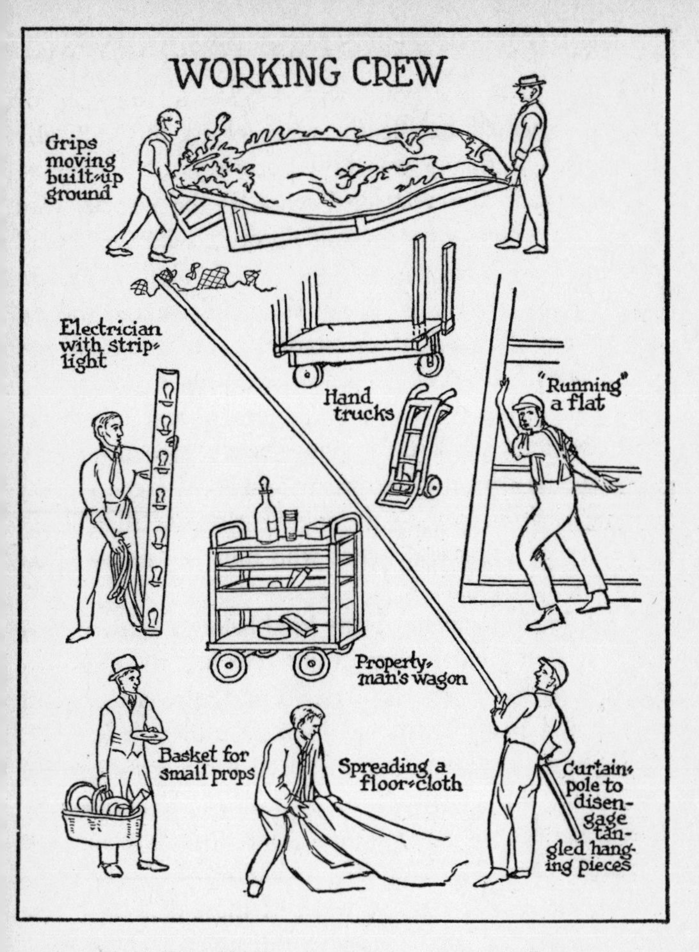

THE THREE DEPARTMENTS OF THE CREW

When Charles Hopkins produced "Treasure Island" at his Punch and Judy Theatre in New York, there were so many stagehands milling about on the tiny stage that he identified them with caps, respectively, red, white and blue.

unions. Until the point was decided no member of the crew would handle the piece or let anybody else touch it. It finally was called scenery.

Scenery, in this restricted sense, is the especial care of the carpenters, or stagehands proper, with the "boss" carpenter as their chief. Their broad subdivisions are into flymen, who work from the gridiron and the fly floors, and "grips," those stationed on or below the stage level. The more skilled men place the pieces, under direction of the head carpenter, and others do the laborious work of moving heavy structures. A carpenter is permitted to repair and build scene pieces; but he is forbidden to do any brushwork, that being the duty of the scenic artist who must be called in as occasion demands.

Lighting equipment of any kind belongs in the jurisdiction of the chief electrician. He has as many assistants as his work requires. For the average small production he ordinarily has just one, although for each arc light of any sort, he is required to have an especial attendant, duly qualified to operate it. Incandescent lamps may be used unattended, and therefore may be remotely controlled from the switchboard.

The better to judge the work of these divisions they must be seen as they function during a performance. The start is with a clear stage because the law generally insists, for reasons of fire hazard, that no set shall be left standing when the theatre is dark. Every person without business in the working area must be out of it before labor begins. Even the actors must be off.

It is observable that the work of all departments is so ordered and timed that all keep going together without interruption. Indeed, the stage crew is usually rehearsed to make sure that its operation will be smooth and rapid. When the place is clear, the stage-hands lay the ground-cloth, the first thing on the scene. While this is being fastened at the edges, if that is necessary (and it is if there is any dancing or running to be done), the property-man and his assistant bring in the heaviest, bulkiest properties and pile them in the middle. Their plan is to work after that from the middle outward, giving the stagehands time and room to set up the walls. But before the walls are closed in —assuming that the set is to be an interior—the ceiling-piece must be lowered from the flies and raised into place, with a line, to lift the chandelier, threaded through in the process. Immediately thereafter, however, flats are brought forward from where they have been stacked, probably against the back wall, and set into position.

Each piece is stenciled with the number of the act (and possibly also of the scene within the act) to which it belongs. If the attraction is touring, the pieces probably also bear the name of the play. Stacks of flats are known as packs, with the further distinction of being either "live" or "dead." The former are the flats that have not yet been used for the performance; the latter are those that have. Handling the flats is sometimes called "running" the packs. To move a flat requires a knack which must be developed in practice; but the method may be described as a way of balancing. Standing back of the flat as it rests upright on the stage floor, the grip grasps the edge of the frame with his left hand just a little above the level of his head, and with his right hand firmly catches one of the lower cross-braces. Inclining the top of the flat toward him so it won't topple away in the opposite direction, he pushes the piece along the stage floor. He doesn't lift it, save as it may catch on an uneven board, but simply slides it into its place.

To the stranger backstage it is a mystery how the stagehands know where to set up isolated pieces that in due time must fit evenly into the set. The explanation is simple. The men have landmarks. The grip finds his key positions from the pieces suspended in the flies, for they will drop accurately into place when they are needed. He "squares" his piece with the cracks in the stage floor which run from the back wall to the footlights. This traditional arrangement of the floor boards is sound, for if they ran the other way the front lighting would show them up distractingly. Of course a floor-cloth is generally used; but the stage worker always anticipates emergencies.

As soon as the walls are set, including such large pieces as heavy mantels or fancy doorways, the electricians, who have connected the chandelier and until now have been bringing up their lamps, cables, and light-stands, begin placing their equipment and connecting the lamps in circuit. The carpenters are still busy tying off their lash-lines and setting their braces, while the property-man, having disposed of his large pieces, is bringing the small objects in on the scene, either in a basket or perhaps on a sort of tea-wagon which he uses as a base of supply. All work industriously together.

In striking the scene the order is generally reversed. The electricians disconnect their lights; the property-man gathers his props into the middle of the scene for removal; the grips carry off the flats and the set pieces; the ceiling-piece is lowered till the chandelier is disengaged and then is hauled vertically upward to its former position in the flies; the property-man vanishes with his charges, and the floor-cloth is rolled up.

When all this work is expertly scheduled, a tremendous amount of detail labor may be accomplished in the brief interval between the acts or in a shorter time if the play requires it. A lot of dust has been stirred up of recent years by persons who declare that the prevailing methods of scene-shifting are clumsy and antiquated; but the fact remains that the old methods are in most circumstances actually quicker than the recommended substitutes. To use a revolving stage or a "wagon" stage or a drop stage or a sliding stage calls for substantial compromises in the design of the setting—many more modifications, it appears, than are demanded by this supposedly obsolete system. It sounds very inviting to build the scene for the second act somewhere at side, or above or below, while Act I is in progress, with one to be slid off and the other on bodily simply by rubbing the Aladdin's lamp of this modern genie Electricity; but the fact is that the trick stages mentioned have more drawbacks than compensations. The simplest of all, the revolving stage, has been tried in many leading theatres of the world; but it rests most of the time in idleness.

These novelties (although they are actually not as great novelties as they seem, having been known for several generations) occupy much space that is not actually required for other purposes. This is the first and, from the artistic standpoint, perhaps the most negligible objection. Next is the fact that the set scene is restricted both as to height and width. But third, and most important, is that they actually do not result in much saving of time over the existing method —not enough to justify all the expense and trouble.

Two of the lately popularized forms have shown practical advantages for especial ends—the wagon stage and the sliding stage. The former was brought most forcefully to American attention by Granville-Barker during his New York repertoire season in 1914-1915. It is not an entire stage. The unit consists of a low platform about six by twelve feet, and sometimes narrower. It is mounted on casters and may be locked to other platforms of the same sort. Scenery is built up on both sides of it, hanging down far enough to cover the casters. To change the scene, the line of interlocking platforms is merely swung about-face.

In an earlier chapter mention was made of the objections to reversible flats. The wagon stage gives the advantage of double-faced flats while using single-faced ones, providing space between to lash them together and brace them. The principal disadvantage is that back and front must be made to conform, an added limitation for the scenic artist who needs all the freedom of expression he can get. It also restricts the use of practical doors and windows, the door-sills having to be as high as the platforms. Moreover, it inflicts a kind of sameness on all the scenes by obliging them to use almost identical elevations. Elevations have their distinct advantages; but like all other devices they should not be overdone.

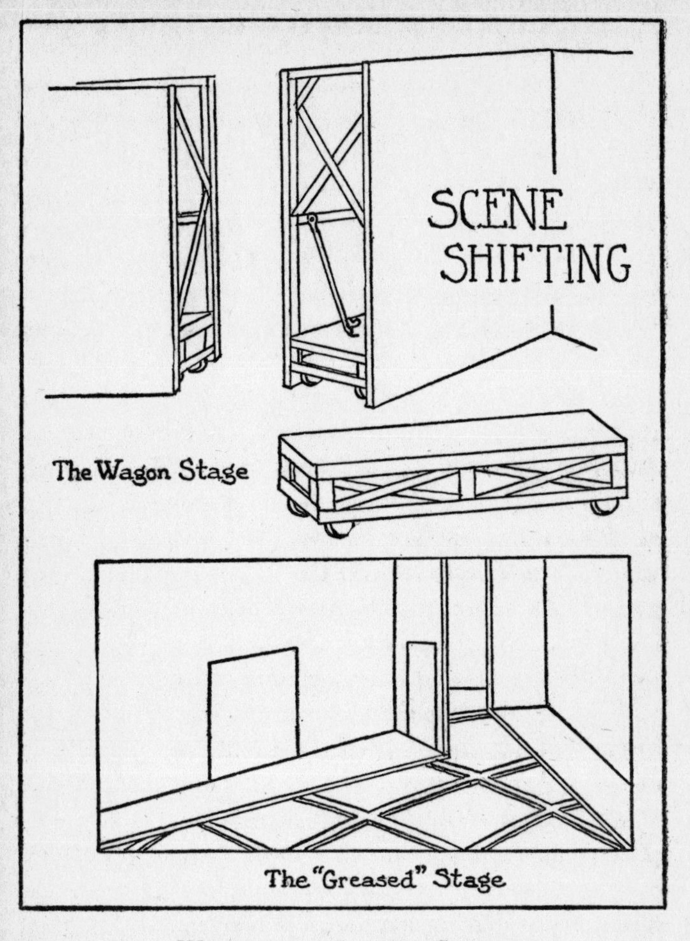

WAGON AND SLIDING STAGES

The wagon stage is simply a small truck with scenery on both sides. When joined with other similar trucks each continuous side makes one complete scene. To change the scene the line is broken and the trucks are turned around. The lower sketch shows the stage arrangement for "The Unknown Purple."

As to the sliding stage, certain plays requiring extraordinarily rapid changes of scene have employed forms of this device when they could be made to fit in with ordinary theatre conditions. "On Trial" was one; "The Unknown Purple" was another. In the case of "On Trial" (produced by Arthur Hopkins) a complete, but necessarily shallow, scene was built on a platform in each of the wings. It was mounted on casters and pivoted at the corner nearest the proscenium arch. First one was turned to fill the picture; then that was turned away that the other might supplant it. In "The Unknown Purple" (produced by Roland West and with Richard Bennett in the leading rôle) the same idea was employed save that a system of stout wooden tracks was laid on the stage floor and thickly greased. The settings themselves were not on casters, but rested directly on the tracks and were pulled into place by a couple of stagehands at a windlass. This play had a third setting which was suspended bodily in the flies and lowered when the other two were away at the sides.

The real problems in scene-shifting are not to transport walls or drops, which may be set at almost incredible speed by ordinary methods, but to move the heavy pieces that cannot safely or conveniently be hung in the flies, or easily moved off at the sides. These heavy parts cared for, prevailing methods are excellent for all else.

If the present book makes any claim to completeness, it is as a sketch of principles involved in operating the world backstage. The whole tale can never be told;

and, indeed, if that were possible it would be a pity—for any record of life to which *finis* may be truly written means that the life it concerns also is at an end. Life in the world behind the scenes goes on and on, and, it is to be hoped, upward. New ways and new means come constantly to the fore. At the same time the old methods endure in so far as they are based upon sound ideas. It is to be doubted that the counterweight system, for instance, now several centuries old as applied to the theatre, ever will be wholly abandoned. So this present sketch, of principles revealed in practice, conceivably may remain true of stage conditions for an extended period.

This concluding chapter is in the nature of summary, a retrospect in which the ground traversed in earlier pages may be viewed with larger perspective. And yet it carries the story on to something new, for, when the details are joined, their combination evolves a separate conception all its own. The total is even greater than the sum of the parts, a very common theatre paradox. The curious means to some ingenious stage effect, the description of which for a time piqued and completely filled the imagination, now falls back into its proper, insignificant place in the scheme without losing its force.

In other words, the way things are done is properly subordinated to what *is* done.

BIBLIOGRAPHY

There seems to be no other running account of precisely the scope of the present work, so recommendations for collateral reading must be haphazard. The matter of stage arrangement will be discussed more intensively in another book on playhouse construction projected for the "American Theatre Manuals" Series. The same is true of the subjects of scene design and lighting, all three to be treated by separate authors, specialists in their lines.

Descriptions of revolving, wagon, sliding, and other more recent stages will be found conveniently in "The Theatre of To-day," by Hiram Kelly Moderwell (New York, 1914, new edition, 1927); Huntley Carter's "The New Spirit in Drama and Art" (New York, 1913), and in J. E. O. Pridmore's article in "The Architectural Review" (November, 1913), "The Mechanical Development of the Modern German Stage." The two last-named include descriptions of the interesting lighting effects of Mariano Fortuny. There should also be mentioned Irving Pichel's "On Building a Theatre" (New York, 1920). A detailed account of Roland West's sliding stage is in the dramatic section of the New York *Times* (December 1, 1918).

The standard general work on the older stages is Edwin O. Sachs's large and fully illustrated "Stage Construction" (London, 1898), this being a supplement to "Modern Opera Houses and Theatres," by the same author in collaboration with E. A. Woodward. An earlier French work of great value is the "Parallèle des principaux théâtres modernes de l'Europe et des machines théâtrales françaises, allemandes et anglaises" (Paris, 1859), text by Joseph de Filippi and drawings by Clement Contant. Georges Moynet's "La machinerie théâtrale—trucs et décors" (Paris, 1893) is an admirable book on backstage in general, profuse in illustrations, many of which show devices for effects.

On the mechanical considerations of scene-painting, it is doubtful that there ever has been written a more useful book than "A Practical Guide to Scene-Painting and Painting in Distemper," by F. Lloyds, one of the ablest scenic artists of his day (London, 1875). The text is authoritative and clear, and so are the illustrations, made by the author. That the considerations have not greatly changed may be seen by comparison of the main points of this book with those named in a talk given by Ernest Albert to "The New York Dramatic Mirror" (November 19, 1913). A separate and rarely-described phase of work on the paint floor may be studied in "English Papièr Mâché," by George Dickinson (London, 1925).

Major works on lighting are a series of articles by Bassett Jones in "The Electrical World" (for the year 1915) entitled "Mobile Color and Stage Lighting," together with one by the same author called "The Possibilities of Stage Lighting" in "The Transactions of the Illuminating Society" (July 20, 1916), and several works by the distinguished lighting engineer, M.

Luckiesh—especially "Color and Its Applications" (New York, 1915), and "Light and Shade" (New York, 1916).

A few random articles are "A New Method of Stage Lighting," by Joseph M. Feeney, in "The Lighting Journal" (New York, October, 1915), describing Belasco's equipment after dispensing with footlights; "John Craig's Notable Undertaking," in "The New York Dramatic Mirror" (May 28, 1913), being an account of the interesting lighting and painting methods of Livingston Platt; "Throwing a New Light on the Drama," by Hugh Ford, in "The Sunday Magazine" of the New York *Tribune* (December 28, 1913), giving the views of a well-known director, and "Psychology of the Stage Switchboard," by Montrose Moses, in "The Theatre Magazine" (New York, August, 1909).

Wells Hawks wrote an article on the stage crew for "The Theatre Magazine" (August, 1904) entitled "Preparing for a New Season," but about all else available on this subject are unimportant press agent squibs in the newspapers. On stage illusions there is much, interspersed through magazines and newspapers for at least a century. "Behind, Below and Above the Scenes" is one interesting account that appeared in "Appleton's Journal" (New York, May 28, 1870). The magazine section of the New York *Times* (November 9, 1913) devoted nearly a page to the record of Lincoln J. Carter in devising effects for many plays. The magazine section of the New York *Tribune* (January 19 of the same year) carried long descriptions of spectacular effects in "The Daughter of

Heaven," "The Whip," "Kismet" and "The Garden of Allah." A fuller account of the last-named production is "Staging a Sandstorm," by Wendell Phillips Dodge, in "The Theatre Magazine" (January, 1912). A long article by Mary B. Mullet in the magazine section of the New York *Sun* (May 20, 1917) discusses mechanical effects from the previously unnoticed angle of how much trouble it takes to make them reasonable.

To see the relationship of all backstage departments to the whole scheme of playhouse operation, the reader is referred to the present author's "Play Production in America" (New York, 1916). Further references are available in William Burt Gamble's fine bibliography, "The Development of Scenic Art and Stage Machinery," prepared for and issued by the New York Public Library (1920, new edition, 1927).

INDEX

Names of authors and titles of works given in the bibliography are omitted from the index. All else, including picture material, is fully keyed.

(1)